CONTENTS

SUMMIT
PRESS

22 Summit Road, Noble Park
Victoria 3174 Australia
Phone: +61 3 9790 5000
Fax: +61 3 9790 6888

This edition first published 2001
Reprinted 2002

This compilation © Summit Press

Editor: Maggie Pinkney
Cover design and formatting: Peter Bourne

Printed in Australia by Griffin Press

National Library of Australia Cataloguing in Publication data

The complete pocket positives, incorporating Pocket positives and More
pocket positives.

ISBN 1 86503 590 4.

1.Quotations. English. 2. Optimism - Quotations, maxims, etc. 3 Success
- Quotations, maxims, etc. I. Title: Pocket positives. II. Title: More
pocket positives.

082

THE COMPLETE

POCKET POSITIVES

Incorporating
Pocket Positives
and
More Pocket Positives

PUBLISHER'S NOTE

The bestselling *Pocket Positives*, compiled by Maggie Pinkney and Barbara Whiter was first published in 1997. Due to its enormous success, a second anthology of inspirational and optimistic quotations, *More Pocket Positives*, was compiled, and published in 1999. Both books are now incorporated here in one volume.

POCKET POSITIVES

Compiled by Maggie Pinkney
and Barbera Whiter

– Introduction –

We all have emotional highs and lows — it's part of being human. The highs aren't a problem, but the lows can take a hold at times, unless we make a conscious effort to get rid of them. This wonderful anthology of 'pocket positives' — small gems of wisdom — provides the key to shaking off the negatives and focusing on life's positive aspects.

These inspirational quotations are a distillation of the benign and healing thoughts of the world's greatest philosophers, poets and mystics, mixed through with the more pithy observations of actors, humorists, novelists, world leaders and exceptional men and women of many other professions. Wherever possible, the dates, nationality and profession of the person quoted is given.

American actress Helen Hayes acknowledged how much we can gain from the reflections of great minds when she wrote:

> We rely upon the poets, the philosophers, and the playwrights to articulate what most of us can only feel, in joy or sorrow. They illuminate the thoughts for which we only grope; they give us the strength and balm we cannot find in ourselves...the wisdom of acceptance and the resilience to push on.

With more than a thousand quotes to choose from, there's something here to suit every occasion — and every mood. It's worth taking a bit of time out every day to dip into and reflect upon these pocket positives — even if you read only one a day. Anyone who takes to heart the wisdom contained in this book will gain a more enlightened, joyful vision of life. As American golfer Walter Hagen so succinctly put it:

> You're only here for a short visit. Don't hurry. Don't worry. And be sure to smell the flowers along the way.

A

— ABILITY —

What lies behind us, and what lies before us are
tiny matters, compared to what lies within us.

Ralph Waldo Emerson (1803-1882)
American essayist, poet and philosopher

When you can do the common things of life in an
uncommon way, you will command the attention
of the world.

Anonymous

God does not ask about your ability.
He asks about your availability.

Anonymous

— ABUNDANCE —

Life is constantly providing us with new funds,
new resources, even when we are reduced to
immobility. In life's ledger there is no such thing
as frozen assets.

Henry Miller (1892-1971)
American author

The world is so full of a number of things,
I'm sure we should all be as happy as kings.

Robert Louis Stevenson (1850-1894)
Scottish novelist, poet and essayist

Develop interest in life as you see it; in people,
things, literature, music — the world is so rich,
simply throbbing with rich treasures, beautiful
souls and interesting people. Forget yourself.

Henry Miller (1891-1980)
American author

— ACCEPTANCE —

God grant me the serenity to accept the things I
cannot change, the courage to change the things I
can, and the wisdom to distinguish the one from
the other.

Reinhold Niebuhr (1892-1971)
American theologian
(Now the prayer of Alcoholics Anonymous)

Acceptance of others, their looks, their
behaviours, their beliefs, brings you an inner
peace and tranquillity — instead of anger
and resentment.

Anonymous

There is no good in arguing with the inevitable.
The only argument available with an east wind is
to put on your overcoat.

James Russell Lowell (1819-1891)
American poet and essayist

— ACCOMPLISH —

If you have accomplished all that you have
planned for yourself, you have not
planned enough.

Edward Everett Hale (1822-1909)
American minister and writer

To accomplish great things we must not only act,
but also dream; not only plan, but also believe.

Anatole France (1844-1924)
French writer

What three things do you want to accomplish
this year? Write them down and place them on
your refrigerator for inspiration all year long.

Anonymous

He that is over-cautious will accomplish little.

Friedrich Von Schiller (1759-1805)
German historian and poet

— ACHIEVE —

If you can walk
You can dance.
If you can talk
You can sing.

Traditional Zimbabwe

Only those who dare to fail greatly can ever
achieve greatly.

Robert F. Kennedy (1925-1968)
American senator and attorney-general

To achieve great things we must live as though
we were never going to die.

Luc de Clapiers, Marquis de Vauvenargues (1715-1747)
French moralist and writer

Achieving starts with believing.

Anonymous

— ACTION —

Doing is better than saying.

Proverb

There are risks and costs to a programme of action, but they are far less than the long-range risks and costs of comfortable inaction.

John F. Kennedy (1917-1963)
President of the United States, 1960-1963

A good plan violently executed right now is far better than a perfect plan executed next week.

General George Patton (1885-1945)
American army general

Deliberation is the work of many men. Action, of one alone.

Charles de Gaulle (1890-1970)
French statesman

Do the thing and you will have the power.

Ralph Waldo Emerson (1803-1882)
American essayist, poet and philosopher

Suit the action to the word, the word to the action; with this special observance, that you o'erstep not the modesty of nature.

William Shakespeare (1564-1616)
English playwright and poet

Keep in mind that, even if you're on the right track, you can still be left behind if you just sit there.

Anonymous

After all is said and done, more is said than done.

Anonymous

Do what you can with what you have,
where you are.

Theodore Roosevelt (1858-1919)
President of the United States, 1901-1912

Action makes more fortunes than caution.

Luc de Clapiers, Marquis de Vauvenargues (1715-1747)
French moralist and writer

Footprints on the sands of time are not made
by sitting down.

Proverb

Actions speak louder than words.

Proverb

Never confuse activity with action.

F. Scott Fitzgerald (1896-1940)
American novelist

It is vain to say human beings might be satisfied with tranquillity; they must have action, and they will make it if they can not find it.

Charlotte Brontë (1816-1855)
English novelist

Those who say a thing cannot be done should not stand in the way of those who are doing it.

Anonymous

Boast not of what thou would'st have done,
but do
What then thou would'st.

John Milton (1606-1674)
English poet

The great end of life is not knowledge, but action.

Thomas Fuller (1608-1661)
English divine and historian

— ADVERSITY —

There is no education like adversity.

Benjamin Disraeli, (1804-1881)
English statesman and writer

Turn your stumbling blocks into stepping stones.

Anonymous

He knows not his own strength that hath not
met adversity.

Ben Jonson (1573-1637)
English dramatist

The stars are constantly shining, but often we do
not see them until the dark hours.

Anonymous

What does not destroy me makes me strong.

Friedrich Wilhelm Nietzche (1844-1900)
German philosopher and critic

Adversity is the state in which man most easily becomes acquainted with himself, being especially free of admirers then.

Samuel Johnson (1709-1784)
English lexicographer, critic and writer

The way I see it, if you want the rainbow, you gotta put up with the rain.

Dolly Parton (1946-)
American singer and songwriter

Adversity has the same effect on a man that severe training has on the pugilist — it reduces him to his fighting weight.

Josh Billings (1818-1885)
American humorist

— ADVICE —

A good scare is worth more than good advice.

Proverb

No-one wants advice — only corroboration.

John Steinbeck (1902~1968)
American novelist

The way of a fool seems right to him, but a wise
man listens to advice.

Proverbs 12:16

Drink nothing without seeing it;
sign nothing without reading it.

Spanish proverb

— AGEING —

Every man desires to live long, but no man would be old.

Jonathan Swift (1667-1745)
English satirist

Do not go gentle into that good night.
Old age should burn and rage at close of day.

Dylan Thomas (1914-1953)
Welsh poet and writer

He who is of a calm and happy nature will hardly feel the pressure of age.

Plato (c.427-c.347 BC)
Greek philosopher

Many people realise their hearts' desires late in life. Continue learning, never stop striving and keep your curiosity sharp, and you will never become too old to appreciate life.

Anonymous

None are so old as those who have
outlived enthusiasm.

Henry David Thoreau (1817-1862)
American essayist, poet and mystic

It's sad to grow old, but nice to ripen.

Brigitte Bardot (1934-)
French actress

The years between fifty and seventy are the
hardest. You are always being asked to do things,
and you are not yet decrepit enough to turn
them down.

T.S. Eliot (1888-1965)
American-born poet and dramatist

One of the many things nobody ever tells you
about middle age is that it's such a nice change
from being young.

Dorothy Canfield Fisher (1879-1958)
American novelist

I prefer old age to the alternative.

Maurice Chevalier (1888~1972)
French singer and actor

As a white candle
In a holy place,
So is the beauty
Of an old face.

Joseph Campbell (1879~1944)
Irish poet

I will never be an old man. To me, old age is
always 15 years older than I am.

Bernard Baruch (1870~1965)
American financier and presidential adviser

Ageing seems to be the only available way to live
a long life.

Daniel-Francois-Esprit Auber (1782~1871)
French composer

One wastes so much time, one is so prodigal of life, at twenty! Our days of winter count for double. That is the compensation of the old.

George Sand (Amandine Aurore Lucie Dupin)
(1804-1876)
French novelist

Old age is like a plane flying through a storm. Once you're aboard, there's nothing you can do. You can't stop the plane, you can't stop the storm, you can't stop time. So one might as well accept it calmly, wisely.

Golda Meir (1898-1978)
Israeli Prime Minister, 1969-1974

Grey hair is great. Ask anyone who's bald.

Lee Trevino (1937-)
American golfer

No wise man ever wished to be younger.

Jonathan Swift (1667-1745)
English satirist

He who keeps a child in his heart never grows old.

Anonymous

Old age is like everything else. To make a success of it, you've got to start young.

Fred Astaire (1899-1987)
American dancer, singer and actor

I look forward to growing old and wise and audacious.

Glenda Jackson (1937-)
English actor and politician

Youth troubles over eternity, age grasps at a day and is satisfied to have even the day.

Dame Mary Gilmore (1865-1962)
Australian poet

Age is not important — unless you are a cheese.

Anonymous

On the whole, I take it that middle age is a
happier period than youth.

Alexander Smith (1830-1867)
Scottish poet

To know how to grow old is the master work of
wisdom, and one of the most difficult chapters in
the great art of living.

Henri Frederic Amiel (1821-1881)
Swiss poet and philosopher

The evening of a well-spent life brings its lamps
with it.

Joseph Joubert (1754-1824)
French writer

— *AMBITION* —

Everybody wants to *be* somebody; nobody wants to *grow*.

Johann Wolfgang von Goethe (1749-1832)
German poet, novelist and playwright

Ah, but a man's reach should exceed his grasp,
Or what's a heaven for?

Robert Browning (1812-1889)
English poet

If you would hit the mark, you must aim a little above it;
Every arrow that flies feels the attraction of earth.

Henry Wadsworth Longfellow (1807-1882)
American poet

No bird soars too high if he soars with his
own wings.

William Blake (1757-1827)
English poet, artist and mystic

When a man is no longer anxious to do better
than well, he is done for.

Benjamin Robert Haydon (1786-1846)
English painter

The rung of a ladder was never meant to rest
upon, but only to hold a man's foot long enough
to enable him to put the other somewhat higher.

Thomas Henry Huxley (1825-1895)
English biologist

★

— ANGER —

I was angry with my friend;
I told my wrath, my wrath did end.
I was angry with my foe;
I told it not, my wrath did grow.

William Blake (1757-1827)
English poet, artist and mystic

Man should forget his anger before he lies down
to sleep.

Thomas de Quincey (1785-1859)
English writer

— ANXIETY —

When you don't have any money, the problem is
food. When you have money, it's sex. When you
have both, it's health. If everything is simply jake,
then you're frightened of death.

James Patrick Donleavy (1926-)
Irish-American writer

— APPEARANCE —

Clothes and manners do not make the man; but
when he is made, they greatly improve
his appearance.

Henry Ward Beecher (1813~1887)
American clergyman

There are no ugly women, only lazy ones.

Helena Rubenstein (1870~1965)
American cosmetics manufacturer

Look successful, be successful.

Proverb

Good temper is one of the great preservers of
the features.

William Hazlitt (1778~1830)
English essayist

— APPRECIATION —

We are so often caught up in our destination that we forget to appreciate the journey, especially the goodness of the people we meet on the way. Appreciation is a wonderful feeling, don't overlook it.

Anonymous

— ASPIRATIONS —

Our aspirations are our possibilities.

Samuel Johnson (1709-1784)
English lexicographer, critic and writer

We can always redeem the man who aspires and tries.

Johann Wolfgang von Goethe (1749-1832)
German poet

— ATTITUDE —

Attitudes are more important than facts.

Norman Vincent Peale (1898-1993)
American writer and minister

A relaxed attitude lengthens a man's life.

Anonymous

We are all in the gutter, but some of us are
looking at the stars.

Oscar Wilde (1854-1900)
Irish poet, wit and dramatist

Nothing is good or bad, but thinking makes it so.

William Shakespeare (1564-1616)
English dramatist and poet

Take the attitude of a student. Never be too big to ask questions. Never know too much to learn something new.

Og Mandino (1923-)
American author

The greatest revolution of our generation is the discovery that human beings, by changing the inner attitudes of their minds, can change the outer aspects of their lives.

William James (1842-1910)
American psychologist and philosopher

If a man does not keep pace with his companions, perhaps it is because he hears a different drummer. Let him step to the music which he hears, however measured or far away.

Henry David Thoreau (1817-1862)
American essayist, poet and mystic

B

— BEAUTY —

People are like stained-glass windows. They sparkle and shine when the sun is out, but when the darkness sets in, their true beauty is revealed only if there is a light from within.

Elisabeth Kubler-Ross (1926-)
Swiss-born American psychiatrist

To look *almost* pretty is an acquisition of higher delight to a girl who has been looking plain for the first fifteen years of her life than a beauty from her cradle can ever receive.

Jane Austen (1775-1817)
English novelist

It is very necessary to have makers of beauty left in a world seemingly bent on making the most evil ugliness.

Vita Sackville-West (1892-1962)
English writer, poet and renowned gardener

Character contributes to beauty. It fortifies a
woman as her youth fades. A mode of conduct,
a standard of courage, discipline, fortitude and
integrity can do a great deal to make a
woman beautiful.

Jacqueline Bisset (1946-)
English actress

Though we travel the world over to find the
beautiful, we must carry it with us or we find
it not.

Ralph Waldo Emerson (1803-1882)
American essayist, poet and philosopher

Things are beautiful if you love them.

Jean Anouilh (1910-1987)
French dramatist

— BEGINNING —

'Tis always morning somewhere in the world.

Richard Henry Horne (1803-1884)
English writer

Whatever you can do or dream you can, begin it.
Boldness has genius, power and magic in it.

Johann Wolfgang von Goethe (1749-1832)
German poet, novelist and playwright

A journey of a thousand miles must begin with a
single step.

Lao-Tze (c.604 BC)
Chinese philosopher and founder of Taoism

All glory comes from daring to begin.

Eugene F. Ware (1841-1911)
American laywyer and verse-writer

— BELIEF —

The secret of making something work in your lives is first of all, the deep desire to make it work: then the faith and belief that it can work: then to hold that clear definite vision in your consciousness and see it working out step by step, without one thought of doubt or disbelief.

Eileen Caddy
Co-founder of The Findhorn Foundation, Scotland

We are what we believe we are.

Benjamin Nathan Cardozo (1870~1938)
American jurist

The thing always happens that you really believe in; and the belief in a thing makes it happen.

Frank Lloyd Wright (1869~1959)
American architect

Believe nothing of what you hear, and only half of what you see.

Proverb

Believe that life is worth living, and your belief will help create the fact.

William James (1842-1910)
American psychologist and philosopher

Whether you believe you can do a thing or believe you can't, you are right.

Henry Ford (1863-1947)
American motor car manufacturer

Belief consists in accepting the affirmations of the soul; unbelief in denying them.

Ralph Waldo Emerson (1803-1882)
American essayist, poet and philosopher

— BEST —

One does not know — cannot know — the best
that is in one.

Friedrich Wilhelm Nietzsche (1844-1900)
German philosopher and critic

It is a funny thing about life; if you refuse to
accept anything but the best, you very often
get it.

W. Somerset Maugham (1874-1965)
English writer

I am easily satisfied with the very best.

Sir Winston Churchill (1874-1965)
English statesman

There is a better way to do it; find it.

Thomas A. Edison (1847-1931)
American inventor

Believe in the best, think your best, study your best, have a goal for your best, never be satisfied with less than your best, try your best, and in the long run things will turn out for the best.

Henry Ford (1863-1947)
American motor car manufacturer

Good, better, best,
May you never rest,
Until your good is better,
And your better best.

Anonymous

Only mediocrity is always at its best.

Max Beerbohm (1872-1956)
English writer and caricaturist

Don't let the best you have done so far be the standard for the rest of your life.

Gustavus F. Swift (1839-1903)
American meat industry magnate

— BIG —

Do not be afraid to take a big step if one is required. You can't cross a chasm in two small jumps.

David Lloyd George (1863-1945)
British Prime Minister, 1916-1922

Think big.

Anonymous

— BIRTHDAYS —

Her birthdays were always important to her, for being a born lover of life, she would always keep the day of her entrance into it as a very great festival indeed.

Elizabeth Goudge (1900-1984)
English author

— BLESSED —

'Tis being and doing and having that make
All the pleasures and pains of which
mankind partake;
To be what God pleases, to do a man's best,
And to have a good heart, is the way to be blest.

Lord Byron (1788-1824)
English poet

Blest, who can unconcern'dly find
Hours, days, and years, slide soft away
In health of body, peace of mind,
Quiet by day,
Sound sleep by night; study and ease
Together mix'd; sweet recreation,
And innocence, which most does please
With meditation.
Thus let me live, unseen unknown;
Thus unlamented let me die;
Steal from the world, and not a stone
Tell where I lie.

Alexander Pope (1688-1744)
English poet

— BLESSING —

May you have food and raiment,
A soft pillow for your head.
May you be half an hour in heaven,
Before the devil knows you're dead.

Traditional Irish

Go, little book, and wish to all
Flowers in the garden, meat in the hall,
A bin of wine, a spice of wit,
A house with lawns enclosing it,
A living river by the door,
A nightingale in the sycamore.

Robert Louis Stevenson (1850-1894)
Scottish novelist, poet and essayist

Now may every living thing, young or old, weak
or strong, living near or far, known or unknown,
living or departed or yet unborn, may every
living thing be full of bliss.

Buddha (5th century BC)
The founder of Buddhism

— BOOKS —

How many a man has dated a new era in his life
from the reading of a book?

Henry David Thoreau (1817-1862)
American essayist, poet and mystic

Make books your companions; let your
bookshelves be your gardens: bask in their
beauty, gather their fruit, pluck their roses, take
their spices and myrrh.

Samuel ben Judah ibn Tibbon (1150-1230)
French-Jewish translator and physician

A good book is the best of friends, the same today
and forever.

Martin Farquhar Tupper (1810-1889)
English writer

It is impossible to mentally or socially enslave a Bible-reading people. The principles of the Bible are the groundwork of human freedom.

Horace Greeley (1811-1872)
American journalist

The New Testament is the very best book that was ever or ever will be known in the world.

Charles Dickens (1812-1870)
English novelist

All that mankind has done, thought, or been is lying in magic preservation in the pages of books.

Thomas Carlyle (1795-1881)
Scottish essayist, historian and philosopher

Books are the quietest and most constant of friends; they are the most accessible and wisest of counsellors, and the most patient of teachers.

Charles W. Eliot (1834-1926)
English educator

We rely upon the poets, the philosophers, and the playwrights to articulate what most of us can only feel, in joy or sorrow. They illuminate the thoughts for which we only grope; they give us the strength and balm we cannot find in ourselves. Whenever I feel my courage wavering I rush to them. They give me the wisdom of acceptance, the will and resilience to push on.

Helen Hayes (1900-1993)
American actress

Literature is my Utopia. Here I am not disenfranchised. No barrier of the sense shuts me out from the sweet, gracious discourses of my book friends. They talk to me without embarrassment or awkwardness.

Helen Keller (1880-1966)
Deaf and blind American lecturer, writer and scholar

— BRAIN —

The chief purpose of the body is to carry the brain around.

Thomas A. Edison (1847-1931)
American inventor

I not only use all the brains I have, but all I can borrow.

Woodrow Wilson (1856-1925)
President of the United States, 1913-1921

— BRAVERY —

Bravery is being the only one who knows you're afraid.

Franklin P. Jones (1832-1902)
American capitalist and politician

— *BRIGHT SIDE* —

No one ever hurt their eyesight by looking at the
bright side of life.

Anonymous

If you can't see the bright side, polish the
dull side.

Anonymous

It is worth a thousand pounds a year to have the
habit of looking on the bright side of things.

Samuel Johnson (1709-1784)
English lexicographer, critic and writer

— BUSINESS —

The secret of business is to know something that
nobody else knows.

Aristotle Socrates Onassis (1906-1975)
Greek shipping magnate

Live together like brothers, but do business
like strangers.

Anonymous

Beware of all enterprises that require
new clothes.

Henry David Thoreau (1817-1862)
American essayist, poet and mystic

Customer service is not a business slogan but a
religion unto itself.

Japanese business philosophy

The happiest time in any man's life is when he is in red-hot pursuit of a dollar, with a reasonable prospect of overtaking it.

Josh Billings (1818-1885)
American humorist

It is not the employer who pays wages — he only handles the money. It is the product that pays wages.

Henry Ford (1863-1947)
American motor car manufacturer

Business should be fun. Without fun, people are left wearing emotional raincoats most of their working lives. Building fun into business is vital; it brings life into our daily being. Fun is a powerful motive for most of our activities and should be a direct path of our livelihood. We should not relegate it to something we buy after work with money we earn.

Michael Phillips (1943 -)
American movie producer

C

— CAREERS —

The best careers advice to give to the young is 'Find out what you like doing best and get someone to pay you for doing it'.

Katharine Whitehorn (1926-)
English newspaper columnist

Never turn a job down because you think it's too small; you don't know where it could lead.

Julia Morgan (1872-1957)
American architect

Plough deep while sluggards sleep.

Benjamin Franklin (1706-1790)
American statesman and philosopher

— CHANGE —

Things do not change: we change.

Henry David Thoreau (1817-1862)
American essayist and poet

★

You can't step into the same river twice.

Heraclitus (c.535-c.475 BC)
Greek philospher

★

If you don't like it, change it. If you don't want to change it, it can't be that bad.

Anonymous

★

Change is a part of every life. Resisting is often as futile as it is frustrating.

Anonymous

Everything flows and nothing stays.

Heraclitus (c.535-c.475 BC)
Greek philospher

Determination, patience and courage are the
only things needed to improve any situation. And,
if you want a situation changed badly enough,
you will find these three things.

Anonymous

We shrink from change; yet is there anything that
can come into being without it? What does
Nature hold dearer, or more proper to herself?
Could you have a hot bath unless the firewood
underwent some change...Is it possible for any
useful thing to be achieved without change? Do
you not see, then, that change in yourself is of the
same order, and no less necessary to Nature?

Marcus Aurelius (121-180 AD)
Roman emperor and philosopher

— CHAOS —

Chaos often breeds life, when order breeds habit.

Henry Brooks Adams (1838~1918)
American historian, journalist and teacher

I say to you: one must have chaos in oneself in order to give birth to a dancing star.

Friedrich Wilhelm Nietzsche (1844~1900)
German philosopher and critic

Out of chaos comes order.

Anonymous

A degree of chaos can be liberating to the creative spirit.

Anonymous

— CHARACTER —

Character consists of what you do on the third
and fourth tries.

James A. Michener (1907-)
American writer

Talent develops in quiet places, character in the
full current of human life.

Johann Wolfgang von Goethe (1749-1832)
German poet, novelist and playwright

In everyone there is something precious, found in
no-one else; so honour each man for what is
hidden within him — for what he alone has, and
none of his fellows.

Hasidic saying

Surely the world we live in is but the world that
lives in us.

Daisy Bates (1836-1915)
Australian social worker

The tree which moves some to tears of joy is, in the eye of others, only a green thing which stands in the way. As a man is, so he sees.

William Blake (1757-1827)
English poet, artist and mystic

In matters of style, swim with the current; in matters of principle, stand like a rock.

Thomas Jefferson (1743-1826)
President of the United States, 1801-1809

A man should endeavour to be as pliant as a reed, yet as hard as cedar wood.

The Talmud

— CHARITY —

With malice toward none, with charity for all.

Abraham Lincoln (1809-1865)
President of the United States, 1861-1865

— CHOICE —

Only she who says
She did not choose, is the loser in the end.

Adrienne Rich (1929-)
American writer

The absence of alternatives clears the
mind marvellously.

Henry Alfred Kissinger (1923-)
German-American statesman and university professor

You can be whatever type of person you choose
to be. Your habits, your behaviours, your
responses, are all your choice.

Anonymous

Happiness or unhappiness is often a matter
of choice.

Anonymous

Only by keeping the past alive in our memories
can we choose what to discard and what to retain
in our present way of life.

Lady (Phyllis Dorothy) Cilento (1894-1987)
Doctor, medical journalist and nutritionist

Every tomorrow has two handles. You can take
hold of the handle of anxiety or the handle of
enthusiasm. Upon your choice so will be the day.

Anonymous

Two roads diverged into a wood, and I —
I took the one less travelled by,
And that has made all the difference.

Robert Frost (1875-1963)
American poet

When you have to make a choice and you don't
make it, that itself is a choice.

William James (1842-1910)
American psychologist and philosopher

— COMFORT —

Whenever I have found that I have blundered or that my work has been imperfect, and when I have been contemptuously criticised and even when I have been overpraised, so that I have felt mortified, it has been my greatest comfort to say hundreds of times to myself that 'I have worked as hard and as well as I could, and no man can do more than this.'

Charles Darwin (1809~1882)
English naturalist

And this for comfort thou must know:
Times that are ill won't still be so;
Clouds will not ever pour down rain;
A sullen day will clear again.

Robert Herrick (1591~1674)
English poet

— COMMITMENT —

We know what happens to people who stay in the middle of the road. They get run over.

Aneurin Bevan (1897-1960)
British Labour politician

In for a penny, in for a pound.

Proverb

I have nothing to offer but blood, toil, tears and sweat.

Sir Winston Churchill (1874-1965)
English statesman

If a job is worth doing, it's worth doing properly.

Proverb

— *COMPROMISE* —

Better bend than break.

Scottish proverb

You cannot shake hands with a clenched fist.

Indira Gandhi (1917~1984)
Indian stateswoman and Prime Minister

— *COMPUNCTION* —

The beginning of compunction is the beginning
of a new life.

George Eliot (Mary Ann Evans) (1819~1880)
English novelist

— CONCENTRATION —

Concentration is my motto. First honesty, then industry, then concentration.

Andrew Carnegie (1835~1919)
Scottish~American industrialist and philanthropist

The shortest way to do many things is to do only one thing at once.

Samuel Smiles (1812-1904)
Scottish author and social reformer

— CONFIDENCE —

Confidence is realising that although you aren't the best at something, you still enjoy doing it.

Anonymous

Confidence is the memory of past success.

Anonymous

— CONSCIENCE —

Conscience: something that feels terrible when everything else feels swell.

Anonymous, from *Reader's Digest*, 1949

Conscience is a cur that will let you get past it, but that you cannot stop from barking.

Anonymous

A man's vanity tells him what is honour; a man's conscience what is justice.

Walter Savage Landor (1775-1864)
English poet and writer

— CONSEQUENCES —

In nature there are neither rewards nor punishments — there are consequences.

Robert Green Ingersoll (1833-1899)
American agnostic

— CONSTANCY —

Plus ça change, plus c'est la même chose. (The more things change, the more they stay the same.)

Alphonse Karr (1808-1890)
French writer

— CONTENTMENT —

Contentment is accepting the world as an imperfect place.

Anonymous

Contentment is not an emotion of incredible highs, because incredible highs always guarantee incredible lows. Contentment is satisfaction over a life that's steady, but fulfilling all the same.

Anonymous

— COURAGE —

Come to the edge, he said.
They said: We are afraid.
Come to the edge, he said.
They came.
He pushed them, and they flew...

Guillaume Apollinaire (1880-1918)
French poet

There is only one courage and that is the courage
to let go of the past, not to collect it, not to
accumulate it, not to cling to it. We all cling to
the past, and because we cling to the past we
become unavailable to the present.

Bhagwan Shree Rajneesh
Indian spiritual cult leader

Courage is what it takes to stand up and speak;
courage is also what it takes to sit down
and listen.

Anonymous

Courage is resistance to fear, mastery of fear, not absence of fear.

Mark Twain (1835-1910)
American writer and humorist

No one has looked back sadly on a life full of experiences, but many look back wishing they had had the courage to do more.

Anonymous

Courage is reckoned the greatest of all virtues, because, unless a man has that virtue, he has no security for preserving any other.

Samuel Johnson (1709-1784)
English lexicographer, critic and writer

What the hell — you might be right, you might be wrong — but don't just avoid.

Katharine Hepburn (1909-)
American actor

★

You gain strength, courage and confidence by every experience in which you really stop to look fear in the face...You must do the thing you cannot do.

Eleanor Roosevelt (1884-1962)
First Lady of the United States, 1933-1945

If the creator had a purpose in equipping us with a neck, he surely meant us to stick it out.

Arthur Koestler (1905-1983)
Hungarian-born writer

What a new face courage puts on everything.

Ralph Waldo Emerson (1803-1883)
American essayist, poet and philosopher

A stout heart breaks bad luck.

Miguel de Cervantes (1547-1616)
Spanish writer

Presence of mind and courage in distress,
Are more than brave armies to procure success.

John Dryden (1631-1700)
English poet and dramatist

Any coward can fight a battle when he's sure of
winning, but give me the man who has pluck to
fight when he's sure of losing.

George Eliot (Mary Ann Evans) (1819-1880)
English novelist

Courage is the price that Life exacts for
granting peace.

Amelia Earhart (1898-1937)
American aviator

Man cannot discover new oceans until he has
courage to lose sight of the shore.

Anonymous

If one is forever cautious, can one remain a
human being?

Alexander Solzhenitsyn (1918-)
Russian writer

— *COURTESY* —

Civility costs nothing.

Proverb

Good manners are made up of petty sacrifices.

Ralph Waldo Emerson (1803-1882)
American essayist, poet and philosopher

Forget the etiquette books. The whole point of
good manners is to put the other person at ease.

Anonymous

— CREATIVITY —

Emptiness is a symptom that you are not living creatively. You either have no goal that is important enough to you, or you are not using your talents and efforts in striving toward an important goal.

Maxwell Maltz
American motivational writer

Creative minds have always been known to survive any kind of bad training.

Anna Freud (1895-1982)
Austrian psychoanalyst

When in doubt, make a fool of yourself. There is a microscopically thin line between being brilliantly creative and acting like the most gigantic idiot on earth. So what the hell, leap.

Cynthia Heimel
American feminist writer (from Village Voice, *1983)*

— CRITICISM —

To avoid criticism, do nothing, say nothing,
be nothing.

Elbert Hubbard (1856-1915)
American writer

Great Spirit, grant that I may not criticize my
neighbour until I have walked a mile in
his moccasins.

American Indian prayer

If you judge people, you have no time to
love them.

Mother Teresa of Calcutta (1910-)
Yugoslav-born missionary

A little self-criticism is as beneficial as too much
is harmful.

Anonymous

If you hear that someone is speaking ill of you, instead of trying to defend yourself, you should say: 'He obviously does not know me very well, since there are so many other faults he could have mentioned.'

Epictetus (c.60–110 AD)
Stoic philosopher

He has the right to criticise, who has a heart to help.

Abraham Lincoln (1809–1865)
President of United States, 1861–1865

— CURIOSITY —

Curiosity is a gift, a capacity of pleasure in knowing, which if you destroy, you make yourselves cold and dull.

John Ruskin (1819-1900)
English author and art critic

A sense of curiosity is nature's original school of education.

Smiley Blanton (1882-1966)
American musician

The important thing is not to stop questioning.

Albert Einstein (1879-1955)
German-born American physicist

Whoever retains the natural curiosity of childhood is never bored or dull.

Anonymous

D

— DEATH —

Death is nothing at all; it does not count. I have only slipped away into the next room.

Canon Henry Scott-Holland (1847-1918)
British cleric

Do not stand at my grave and weep;
I am not there. I do not sleep.
I am a thousand winds that blow.
I am the diamond glints on snow.
I am the sunlight on ripened grain.
I am the gentle autumn's rain.
When you awaken in the morning's hush,
I am the swift uplifting rush
Of quiet birds in circled flight.
I am the soft stars that shine at night.
Do not stand at my grave and cry;
I am not there. I did not die.

Anonymous

It matters not how a man dies, but how he lives. The act of dying is not of importance, it lasts so short a time.

Samuel Johnson (1709-1784)
English lexicographer, critic and writer

It is better to die on your feet than live on your knees.

Dolores Ibarruri (1895-1989)
Spanish communist leader and orator

Death can show us the way, for when we know and understand completely that our time on this earth is limited, and that we have no way of knowing when it will be over, then we must live each day as if it were the only one we had.

Elisabeth Kubler-Ross (1926-)
Swiss-born American psychiatrist

To fear death, gentlemen, is nothing other than to think oneself wise when one is not; for it is to think one knows what one does not know. No man knows whether death may not even turn out to be the greatest of blessings for a human being; and yet people fear it as if they knew for certain that it is the greatest of evils.

Socrates (c.469~399 BC)
Greek philosopher

As a goldsmith, taking a piece of gold transforms it into another newer and more beautiful form, even so this self, casting off this body and dissolving its ignorance, makes for itself another newer and more beautiful form.

Brhadaranyaka IV:43-4

Death is but crossing the world, as friends do the seas; they live in one another still.

William Penn (1644~1718)
English Quaker and founder of Pennsylvania, USA

What will survive of us is love.

Philip Larkin (1922-1985)
English poet

Thinking about death...produces love for life.
When we are familiar with death, we accept
each week, each day, as a gift. Only if we are able
thus to accept life — bit by bit — does it
become precious.

Albert Schweitzer (1875-1965)
Alsatian medical missionary

The years seem to rush by now, and I think of
death as a fast approaching end of a journey —
double and treble the reason for loving as well as
working while it is day.

George Eliot (Mary Ann Evans) (1819-1880)
English novelist

Death is the final stage of growth in this life.
There is no total death. Only the body dies. The
self or spirit, or whatever you may wish to label
it, is eternal.

Elisabeth Kubler-Ross (1926-)
Swiss-born American psychiatrist

To die completely, a person must not only forget
but be forgotten, and he who is not forgotten is
not dead.

Samuel Butler (1835-1902)
English writer and satirist

When we truly love, it is never lost. It is only
after death that the depth of the bond is truly felt,
and our loved one becomes more a part of us
than was possible in life.

Oriental tradition

— DECISIONS —

You don't drown by falling in the water. You
drown by staying there.

Anonymous

No trumpets sound when the important
decisions of our life are made. Destiny is
made known silently.

Agnes de Mille (1908-)
American choreographer

Whenever you see a successful business,
someone once made a courageous decision.

Peter Drucker (1909-)
American management consultant

— DEEDS —

Our grand business in life is not to see what lies dimly at a distance, but to do what lies clearly at hand.

Thomas Carlyle (1795-1881)
Scottish essayist, historian and philosopher

A man can only do what he can do. But if he does that each day he can sleep at night and do it again the next day.

Albert Schweitzer (1875-1965)
Alsatian medical missionary

By his deeds we know a man.

African proverb

What counts in life is not what you say but what you do.

Anonymous

A deed knocks first at Thought
And then — it knocks at Will —
That is the manufacturing spot.

Emily Dickinson (1830-1886)
American poet

Our deeds travel with us from afar, and what we
have been makes us what we are.

George Eliot (Mary Ann Evans) (1819-1880)
English novelist

The shortest answer is doing.

English Proverb

Every thought I have imprisioned in expression I
must free by my deeds.

Kahlil Gibran (1883-1931)
Lebanese writer, artist and mystic

— DEFEAT —

Do not be afraid of defeat. You are never so near
victory as when defeated in a good cause.

Henry Ward Beecher (1813-1887)
American clergyman

★

— DELIGHT —

Among the mind's powers is one that comes of
itself to many children and artists. It need not be
lost, to the end of his days, by anyone who has
ever had it. This is the power of taking delight in
a thing, or rather in anything, not as a means to
some other end, but just because it is what it is. A
child in the full health of his mind will put his
hand flat on the summer lawn, feel it, and give a
little shiver of private glee at the elastic firmness
of the globe.

Charles Edward Montague (1867-1928)
English novelist and essayist

— DESIRE —

Lord, grant that I may always desire more than I can accomplish.

Michelangelo (1474-1564)
Italian sculptor, painter and poet

Desires are only the lack of something: and those who have the greatest desires are in a worse condition than those who have none, or very slight ones.

Plato (c.427-347 BC)
Greek philosopher

Desire is the very essence of man.

Benedict Spinoza (1632-1677)
Dutch philosopher

— DESPAIR —

Despair doubles our strength.

French proverb

It is always darkest just before the day dawneth.

Thomas Fuller (1608-1661)
English divine and historian

When we are flat on our backs there is no way to look but up.

Roger W. Babson (1875-1967)
American economist

In the midst of winter, I finally learned that there was in me an invincible summer.

Albert Camus (1913-1960)
French writer

— DESTINY —

To live content with small means; to seek
elegance rather than luxury, and refinement
rather than fashion; to be worthy, not
respectable, and wealthy, not rich; to study
hard, think quietly, talk gently, act frankly; to
listen to stars and birds, to babes and sages, with
open heart; to bear all cheerfully, do all bravely,
await occasions, hurry never. In a word to let the
spiritual, unbidden and unconscious, grow up
through the common. This is to be
my symphony.

William Ellery Channing (1780-1842)
American minister

If thou follow thy star, thou canst not fail of a
glorious haven.

Dante Alighieri (1265-1321)
Italian poet, statesman and diplomat

Destiny: a tyrant's excuse for crime and a fool's excuse for failure.

Ambrose Bierce (1842-1911)
American journalist

Destiny is not a matter of chance, it is a matter of choice.

William Jennings Bryan (1860-1925)
American lawyer and politician

Everything that happens happens as it should, and if you observe carefully, you will find this to be so.

Marcus Aurelius (121-180 AD)
Roman emperor and philosopher

We are not creatures of circumstance; we are creators of circumstance.

Benjamin Disraeli (1804-1881)
English statesman and writer

— DIFFICULTY —

All things are difficult before they are easy.

Thomas Fuller (1608~1661)
English divine and historian

The hill, though high, I covet to ascend;
The difficulty will not offend,
For I perceive the way to life lies here.
Come, pluck up heart, let's neither faint nor fear;
Better, though difficult, the right way to go,
Than wrong, though easy,
Where the end is woe.

John Bunyan (1628~1688)
English writer and moralist

Keep the faculty of effort alive in you by a little
gratuitous exercise every day. That is be
systematically heroic in little unnecessary points,
do every day or two something for no other
reason than its difficulty.

William James (1842~1910)
American psychologist and philosopher

— *DIRECTION* —

I can't change the direction of the wind. But I can adjust my sails.

Anonymous

Determine on some course, more than a wild exposure to each chance.

William Shakespeare (1564-1616)
English playwright and poet

The thing has already taken form in my mind before I start it. The first attempts are absolutely unbearable. I say this because I want you to know that if you see something worthwhile in what I am doing, it is not by accident but because of real direction and purpose.

Vincent van Gogh (1853-1890)
Dutch post-impressionist painter

— DISCIPLINE —

Discipline is the soul of an army. It makes small numbers formidable, procures success to the weak, and esteem to all.

George Washington (1732-1799)
First President of the United States, 1789-1797

— DISCOVERY —

The real voyage of discovery consists not in seeking new landscapes but in having new eyes.

Marcel Proust (1871-1922)
French novelist

Discovery consists of seeing what everybody has seen and thinking what nobody has thought.

Albert Szent-Györgyi (1893-unknown)
Hungarian-born American biochemist

— DREAMS —

Dreams don't have to come true by age 20, 30 or 40: they often occur long past when you thought possible.

Anonymous

All big men are dreamers. They see things in the soft haze of a spring day or in the red fire of a long winter's evening. Some of us let great dreams die, but others nourish and protect them, nurse them through bad days till they bring them to the sunshine and light which comes always to those who sincerely hope that their dreams will come true.

Woodrow Wilson (1856-1925)
President of the United States, 1913-1921

Some men see things as they are and say 'Why?' I dream things that never were, and say, 'Why not?'

George Bernard Shaw (1856-1950)
Irish dramatist, essayist and critic

Go confidently in the direction of your dreams!
Live the life you've imagined.

Henry David Thoreau (1817-1862)
American essayist, poet and mystic

If you have built castles in the air, your work
need not be lost; that is where they should be.
Now put the foundations under them.

Henry David Thoreau (1817-1862)
American essayist, poet and mystic

Take your dream, attach it to a star and never
lose it. If you lose it...you've lost your
enthusiasm; you've settled for something less.
This will never do. Fight like hell for your
dream and get it.

Guru RHH

If there were dreams to sell,
What would you buy?
Some cost a passing-bell;
Some a light sigh.

Thomas Lovell Beddoes (1803-1849)
English poet and physiologist

Those who dream by day are cognizant of many
things which escape those who dream only
by night.

Edgar Allan Poe (1809-1849)
American poet and writer

Dreams are the touchstones of our characters.

Henry David Thoreau (1817-1862)
American essayist, poet and mystic

The future belongs to those who believe in the
beauty of their dreams.

Eleanor Roosevelt (1884-1962)
First Lady of the United States, 1933-1945

Who looks outside dreams; who looks
inside wakes.

Carl Jung (1875-1961)
Swiss psychiatrist

All men dream, but not equally. Those who
dream by night in the dusty recesses of their
minds wake in the day to find that it was vanity:
but the dreamers of the day are dangerous men,
for they may act their dream with open eyes, to
make it possible.

T.E. Lawrence (Lawrence of Arabia) (1888-1935)
English soldier and writer

My dreams were all my own; I accounted for
them to nobody; they were my refuge when
annoyed — my dearest pleasure when free.

Mary Shelley (1797-1851)
English author

Learning to understand our dreams is a matter of learning to understand our heart's language.

Anne Faraday (1935-)
American psychologist and dream researcher

An uninterpreted dream is like an unopened letter.

Jewish proverb

— *DURABILITY* —

The more I study the world, the more I am convinced of the inability of brute force to create anything durable.

Napoleon Bonaparte I (1769-1821)
French emperor

★

E

– EDUCATION –

Education is simply the soul of a society as it passes from one generation to another.

G.K. Chesterton (1874-1936)
English writer

If you educate a man you educate a person, but if you educate a woman you educate a family.

Ruby Manikan (20th century)
Indian church leader

— ENDURANCE —

Nothing happens to any man that he is not
formed by nature to bear.

Marcus Aurelius (121-180 BC)
Roman emperor and philosopher

Endure, and keep yourself for days of happiness

Virgil (70-19 BC)
Roman poet

We could never learn to be brave and patient if
there were only joy in the world.

Helen Keller (1880-1968)
Deaf and blind American lecturer, writer and scholar

No pain, no palm; no thorns, no throne; no gall,
no glory; no cross, no crown.

William Penn (1644-1718)
English Quaker and founder of Pennsylvania, USA

— ENEMIES —

Beware of no man more than yourself; we carry our worst enemies within us.

Charles Haddon Spurgeon (1834-1892)
English clergyman

— ENERGY —

If an unusual necessity forces us onward, a surprising thing occurs. The fatigue gets worse up to a certain point, when, gradually or suddenly, it passes away and we are fresher than before! We have evidently tapped a new level of energy. There may be layer after layer of this experience, a third and fourth wind. We find amounts of ease and power that we never dreamed ourselves to own, sources of strength habitually not taxed, because habitually we never push through the obstruction of fatigue.

William James (1842-1910)
American psychologist and philosopher

— ENJOYMENT —

At the judgement day a man will be called to account for all the good things he might have enjoyed and did not enjoy.

Jewish proverb

He neither drank, smoked, nor rode a bicycle. Living frugally, saving his money, he died early, surrounded by greedy relatives. It was a great lesson to me.

John Barrymore (1882-1942)
American actor

— ENTHUSIASM —

Nothing great was ever achieved
without enthusiasm.

Ralph Waldo Emerson (1803-1882)
American essayist, poet and philosopher

None so old as those who have
outlived enthusiasm.

Henry David Thoreau (1817-1862)
American poet, essayist and mystic

If you are not getting as much from life as you
want to, then examine the state of
your enthusiasm.

Norman Vincent Peale (1898-1993)
American writer and minister

The person who loves always
becomes enthusiastic.

Norman Vincent Peale (1898~1993)
American writer and minister

Act enthusiastic and you become enthusiastic.

Dale Carnegie (1888~1955)
American author and lecturer

You can do anything if you have
enthusiasm...Enthusiasm is at the bottom of all
progress. With it, there is accomplishment.
Without it, there are only alibis.

Henry Ford (1863~1947)
American motor car manufacturer

No man who is enthusiastic about his work has
anything to fear from life.

Samuel Goldwyn (1882~1974)
American film producer

Do not be afraid of enthusiasm. You need it. You can do nothing effectively without it.

Francois Pierre Guillaume Guizot (1787-1874)
French historian and statesman

The love of life is necessary to the vigorous prosecution of any undertaking.

Samuel Johnson (1709-1784)
English lexicographer, critic and writer

We act as though comfort and luxury were the chief requirements of life, when all that we need to make us really happy is something to be enthusiastic about.

Charles Kingsley (1819-1875)
English writer and clergyman

— EXCELLENCE —

Excellence is to do a common thing in an
uncommon way.

Booker Taliaferio Washington (1856-1915)
American teacher, writer and speaker

— EXCUSES —

He that is good at making excuses is seldom good
at anything else.

Benjamin Franklin (1706-1790)
American statesman and philospher

The trick is not how much pain you feel — but
how much joy you feel. Any idiot can feel pain.
Life is full of excuses to feel pain, excuses not to
live, excuses, excuses, excuses.

Erica Jong (1942-)
American novelist and poet

— EXPERIENCE —

Experience is not what happens to a man. It is
what a man does with what happens to him.

Aldous Huxley (1894-1963)
English novelist and essayist

Nothing ever becomes real till it is experienced.
Even a proverb is no proverb to you till your life
has illustrated it.

John Keats (1795-1821)
English poet

And other's follies teach us not,
Nor much their wisdom teaches,
And most, of sterling worth, is what
Our own experience teaches.

Alfred, Lord Tennyson (1809-1892)
English poet

Experience is the name everyone gives to
their mistakes.

Oscar Wilde (1854-1900)
Irish poet, wit and dramatist

Experience is a hard teacher because she gives
the test first, the lesson afterwards.

Vernon Sanders Law

The art of living is the art of using experience —
your own and other people's.

Herbert Louis Samuel (1870-1963)
British politician and administrator

Experience isn't interesting till it begins to repeat
itself — in fact, till it does that, it hardly
is experience.

Elizabeth Bowen (1899-1973)
Irish novelist

A moment's insight is sometimes worth a life's experience.

Oliver Wendell Holmes (1809~1894)
American writer

Experience is one thing you can't get for nothing.

Oscar Wilde (1854~1900)
Irish poet, wit and dramatist

— *EXTRAORDINARY* —

The difference between ordinary and extraordinary is that little extra.

Anonymous

F

– FAILURE –

When we begin to take our failures
non-seriously, it means we are ceasing to be
afraid of them. It is of immense importance to
learn to laugh at ourselves.

Katherine Mansfield (1888-1923)
New Zealand author

If at first you don't succeed you're running
about average.

Margaret H. Alderson *(1959-)*
Journalist

A failure is a man who has blundered, but is not
able to cash in on the experience.

Elbert Hubbard (1856-1915)
American writer

He who never fails will never grow rich.

Charles Haddon Spurgeon (1834-1892)
English clergyman

We are all of us failures — at least the best of us are.

J.M. Barrie (1860-1937)
Scottish writer

He's no failure. He's not dead yet.

Gwilym Lloyd George (1894-1967)
Welsh politician

Say not that she did well or ill,
Only 'She did her best'.

Dinah Maria Craik (1826-1887)
English novelist and poet

If men could regard the events of their lives with more open minds they would frequently discover that they did not really desire the things they failed to obtain.

André Maurois (1885-1967)
French writer

We learn wisdom from failure much more than success. We often discover what we WILL do, by finding out what we will NOT do.

Samuel Smiles (1812-1904)
Scottish author and social reformer

There is only one real failure in life that is possible and that is, not to be true to the best one knows.

Frederic Farrer (1831-1903)
English clergyman and writer

— FAITH —

Be still, sad heart! and cease repining;
Behind the clouds is the sun still shining;
Thy fate is the common fate of all,
Into each life some rain must fall.

Henry Wadsworth Longfellow (1807-1882)
American poet

They can because they think they can.

Virgil (70-19 BC)
Roman poet

Without winter, there can be no spring.
Without mistakes, there can be no learning.
Without doubts, there can be no faith.
Without fears, there can be no courage.
My mistakes, my fears and my doubts are my
path to wisdom, faith and courage.

Anonymous

I feel no need for any other faith than my faith in human beings.

Pearl S. Buck (1892~1973)
American novelist

In the midst of outer dangers I have felt an inner calm and known resources of strength that only God could give. In many instances I have felt the power of God transforming the fatigue of despair into the buoyancy of hope. I am convinced that the universe is under the control of a loving purpose and that in the struggle for righteousness man has cosmic companionship. Behind the harsh appearances of the world there is a benign power.

Martin Luther King (1929~1968)
American black civil-rights leader

Proof is the last thing looked for by a truly religious mind which feels the imaginative fitness of its faith.

George Santayana (1863~1952)
Spanish~American philosopher and poet

Dame Edith Sitwell, when asked why she had come to faith, said she had looked at the pattern of a frosted flower on a window-pane, she had studied shells, feathers, petals and grasses, and she knew without doubt there must be a cause...

Quoted in *Christian Poetry*

He who sees the Infinite in all things sees God.

William Blake (1757-1827)
English poet, artist and mystic

I believe in God and in nature and in the triumph of good over evil.

Johann Wolfgang von Goethe (1749-1832)
German poet, novelist and playwright

If you have abandoned one faith, do not abandon all faith. There is always an alternative to the faith we lose. Or could it be the same thing under another mask?

Graham Greene (1904-1991)
English novelist

— FATE —

Whatever fate befalls you, do not give way to great rejoicing, or great lamentation...All things are full of change, and your fortunes may turn at any moment.

Arthur Schopenhauer (1788-1860)
Philosopher

Lots of folks confuse bad management with destiny.

Frank McKinney Hubbard (1868-1930)

I do not believe in a fate that falls on men however they act; but I do believe in a fate that falls on them unless they act.

G.K. Chesterton (1874-1936)
English writer

— FAULTS —

When you have faults, do not fear to
abandon them.

Confucius (551~479 BC)
Chinese philosopher

We all have faults. It's important to recognise
your own, but to try and turn a blind eye to the
faults of others.

Anonymous

Love your enemies, for they tell you your faults.

Benjamin Franklin (1706-1790)
American statesman and philosopher

— *FEAR* —

Fear is never a reason for quitting: it is only
an excuse.

Norman Vincent Peale (1898~1993)
American writer and minister

To fear love is to fear life, and those who fear life
are already three parts dead.

Bertrand Russell (1872~1970)
English philosopher and mathematician

Do the thing you fear and the death of fear
is certain.

Ralph Waldo Emerson (1803~1882)
American essayist, poet and philosopher

There is no fear in love; but perfect love casteth
out fear: because fear hath torment. He that
feareth is not made perfect in love.

1 John 4:18

Nothing in life is to be feared. It is only to
be understood.

Marie Curie (1867–1934)
French physicist

Let me assert my firm belief that the only things
we have to fear is fear itself.

Franklin D. Roosevelt (1882–1945)
President of the United States, 1932–1945

To conquer fear is the beginning of wisdom, in
the pursuit of truth as in the endeavour after a
worthy manner of life.

Bertrand Russell (1872–1970)
English philosopher and mathematician

Considering how dangerous everything is
nothing is really very frightening.

Gertrude Stein (1874–1946)
American author

Of all the liars in the world, sometimes the worst are your own fears.

Rudyard Kipling (1865-1936)
English poet and author

When I became ill, the years of pain and confusion loomed up like some primitive monster of the deep. I had to face the monster or drown. There were many nights when I thought I was going under for the last time. I lived in fear of dying. The strange paradox is that by confronting my fear of death, I found myself and created a new life.

Lucia Capacchione
American art therapist and pioneer in inner healing

Carry your own lantern and you need not fear the dark.

*Leo Rosten's Treasury of Jewish
Quotations*

— *FORGIVENESS* —

Forgive your enemies, but never forget
their names.

John F. Kennedy (1917~1963)
President of the United States, 1961~1963

Lift up your eyes and look on one another in
innocence born of complete forgiveness of each
other's illusions.

A Course in Miracles

The forgiving state of mind is a magnetic power
for attracting good. No good thing can be
withheld from the forgiving state of mind.

Catherine Ponder
American motivational writer

To err is human, to forgive, divine.

Alexander Pope (1688-1744)
English poet

The reason to forgive is for your own sake. For
our own health Because beyond that point
needed for healing, if we hold onto our anger, we
stop growing and our souls begin to shrivel.

M. Scott Peck (1936-)
American psychiatrist and writer

One forgives as much as one loves.

Francois, Duc de La Rochefoucauld (1616-1680)
French writer

Sometimes the hardest person to forgive is
yourself. But we shouldn't be harder on ourselves
than we would be on others.

Anonymous

— FREEDOM —

Once freedom lights its beacon in a man's heart,
the gods are powerless against him.

Jean-Paul Sartre (1905-1980)
French writer

I disapprove of what you say, but I will defend to
the death your right to say it.

Voltaire (1694-1778)
French author

The moment the slave resolves that he will no
longer be a slave, his fetters fall. He frees himself
and shows the way to others. Freedom and
slavery are mental states.

Mahatma Gandhi (1869-1948)
Indian leader, moral teacher and reformer

Freedom is the right to tell people what they do not want to hear.

George Orwell (1903-1950)
English novelist

Man is free at the moment he wishes to be.

Voltaire (1694-1778)
French writer

You only have power over people so long as you don't take everything away from them. But when you've robbed a man of everything he's no longer in your power — he's free again.

Alexander Solzhenitsyn (1918-)
Russian writer

Freedom's just another word for nothing left to lose.

Kris Kristofferson (1936-)
American actor and folk singer

The most beautiful thing in the world is freedom of speech.

Diogenes (412?-323 BC)
Greek philosopher

Liberty, when it begins to take root, is a plant of rapid growth.

George Washington (1732-1799)
First President of the United States, 1789-1797

Liberty means responsibility. That is why most dread it.

George Bernard Shaw (1856-1950)
Irish dramatist, essayist and critic

The love of liberty is the love of others.
The love of power is the love of ourselves.

William Hazlitt (1778-1830)
English essayist

— FRIENDS —

Your friend is the man who knows all about you,
and still likes you.

Elbert Hubbard (1856-1915)
American writer

The only way to have a friend is to be one.

Ralph Waldo Emerson (1803-1882)
American essayist, poet and philosopher

Friendship is always a sweet responsibility, never
an opportunity.

Kahlil Gibran (1883-1931)
Lebanese poet, writer, artist and mystic

So long as we are loved by others I should say
that we are almost indispensable; and no man is
useless while he has a friend.

Robert Louis Stevenson (1850-1894)
Scottish novelist, poet and essayist

Slender at first, they quickly gather force,
Growing in richness as they run their course;
Once started, they do not turn back again:
Rivers, and years, and friendships with good men.

Sanskrit poem

Don't sacrifice your life to work and ideals. The
most important things in life are human
relations. I found that out too late.

Katharine Susannah Prichard (1883-1969)
Australian author

Am I not destroying my enemies when I make
friends of them?

Abraham Lincoln (1809-1865)
President of the United States, 1861-1865

A man who turns his back on his friends soon
finds himself facing a very small audience.

Dick Powell (1904-1963)
American actor

No man is wise enough by himself.

Titus Maccius Plautus (250-184 BC)
Roman poet and comic playwright

Forsake not an old friend; for the new is not
comparable to him: a new friend is as new wine;
when it is old, thou shalt drink it with pleasure.

Ecclesiastes

Instead of loving your enemies treat your friends
a little better.

E.W. Howe (1853-1937)
American novelist

Friendship consists in forgetting what one gives,
and remembering what one receives.

Alexandré Dumas (1803-1870)
French novelist

He that is a friend to himself, know; he is a friend to all.

Montaigne (1533-1592)
French essayist

Animals are such agreeable friends — they ask no questions, they pass no criticisms.

George Eliot (Mary Ann Evans) 1819-1880
English novelist

Be a friend to thyself and others will too.

Thomas Fuller (1608-1661)
English divine and historian

What is a friend? A single soul dwelling in two bodies.

Aristotle (384-322 BC)
Greek philosopher

The thread of our life would be dark,
Heaven knows!
If it were not with friendship and love
intertwined.

Thomas Moore (1779-1852)
Irish poet

Where there are friends, there is wealth.

Titus Maccius Plautus (250-184 BC)
Roman poet and comic playwright

They are rich who have true friends.

Thomas Fuller (1608-1661)
English divine and historian

Friendship is a sheltering tree.

Samuel Taylor Coleridge (1772-1834)
English poet

Friendship is the gift of the gods, and the most precious boon to man.

Benjamin Disraeli (1804-1881)
English statesman and author

You can always tell a real friend: when you've made a fool of yourself he doesn't feel you've done a permanent job.

Laurence J. Peter (1918-)
Canadian writer

The light of friendship is like the light of phosphorus, even plainest when all around is dark.

Grace Crowell (1877-1969)
American poet

— FULFILMENT —

Fulfilment is deciding what you want out of life, and working towards it. Fulfilment is not merely the reaching of a specific destination.

Anonymous

Fulfilment is reaching your own expectations, not the expectations of others.

Anonymous

It is never too late to be what you might have been.

George Eliot (Mary Ann Evans)
(1819-1880)
English novelist

— FUTURE —

I am not interested in the past. I am interested in the future, for that is where I expect to spend the rest of my life.

Charles Franklin Kettering (1876-1958)
American engineer and inventor

Future — that period of time in which our affairs prosper, our friends are true and our happiness is assured.

Ambrose Bierce (1842-1914)
American writer

What are you looking forward to in the next year? The next ten years? Isn't it exciting to imagine all the possibilities the future holds?

Anonymous

Never let the future disturb you. You will meet it,
if you have to, with the same weapons of reason
which today arm you against the present.

Marcus Aurelius (121-180 AD)
Roman emperor and philosopher

The best thing about the future is that it comes
only one day at a time.

Abraham Lincoln (1809-1865)
President of United States, (1861-1865)

To most of us the future seems unsure; but then it
always has been, and we who have seen great
changes must have great hopes.

John Masefield (1878-1967)
English poet

G

— GARDENS —

Who loves a garden still his Eden keeps,
Perennial pleasures, plants and wholesome
harvest reaps.

Amos Bronson Alcott (1799-1888)
American teacher and philosopher

Yes, in the poor man's garden grow
Far more than herbs and flowers —
Kind thoughts, contentments, peace of mind,
And joy for weary hours.

Mary Howitt (1799-1888)
English author

He who has roses in his garden also has roses in
his heart.

Anonymous

I scorn the doubts and cares that hurt
The world and all its mockeries,
My only care is now to squirt
The ferns among my rockeries.
In early youth and later life
I've seen an up and seen a down,
And now I have a loving wife
To help me peg verbena down.

In peace and quiet pass our days,
With nought to vex our craniums,
Our middle beds are all ablaze
With red and white geraniums.

...

Let him who'd have the peace he needs
Give all his worldly mumming up,
Then dig a garden, plant the seeds,
And watch the product coming up.

George R. Sims (1847-1922)
English poet

One is nearer God's Heart in a garden,
Than anywhere else on earth.

Dorothy Frances Gurney (1858-1932)
English poet

— GENIUS —

Genius is one per cent inspiration and
ninety-nine per cent perspiration.

Thomas A. Edison (1847-1931)
American inventor

One is not born a genius, one becomes a genius.

Simone de Beauvoir (1908-1986)
French writer

Genius is nothing but labour and diligence.

William Hogarth (1697-1764)
English painter and political caricaturist

To believe your own thought, to believe that what
is true for you in your private heart is true for all
men — that is genius.

Ralph Waldo Emerson (1803-1882)
American essayist, poet and philosopher

— GIFTS —

You are surrounded by gifts every living moment
of every day. Let yourself feel appreciation for
their presence in your life and take the time to
acknowledge their splendour.

Lon G. Nungesser
Writer

Earth's crammed with heaven,
And every common bush afire with God.

Elizabeth Barrett Browning (1806-1861)
English poet

O gift of God! a perfect day,
Whereon shall no man work but play,
Whereon it is enough for me
Not to be doing but to be.

Henry Wadsworth Longfellow (1807-1882)
American poet

— GIVING —

You give but little when you give of your possessions. It is when you give of yourself that you truly give.

Kahlil Gibran (1883-1931)
Lebanese poet, writer, artist and mystic

The only gift is a portion of thyself.

Ralph Waldo Emerson (1803-1882)
American essayist, poet and philosopher

The manner of giving is worth more than the gift.

Pierre Corneille (1606-1684)
French dramatist

Every man according as he purposeth in his heart, so let him give; not grudgingly, or out of necessity: for God loveth a cheerful giver.

Corinthians 9:7

135

— GOALS —

You have to know what you want to get. But when you know that, let it take you. And if it seems to take you off the track, don't hold back, because perhaps that is instinctively where you want to be. And if you hold back and try to be always where you have been before, you will go dry.

Gertrude Stein (1874-1946)
American writer

One can never consent to creep when one feels an impulse to soar.

Helen Keller (1880-1968)
Deaf and blind American lecturer, writer and scholar

Shoot for the moon. Even if you miss it you will land among the stars.

Les (Lester Louis) Brown (1928-)
Journalist

All successful people have a goal. No one can get anywhere unless he knows where he wants to go and what he wants to be or do.

Norman Vincent Peale (1898-1993)
American writer and minister

A man without a purpose is like a ship without a rudder.

Thomas Carlyle (1795-1881)
Scottish essayist, historian and philosopher

The world stands aside for he who knows where he is going.

Proverb

The significance of a man is not in what he attains, but rather in what he longs to attain.

Kahil Gibran (1883-1931)
Lebanese writer, artist and mystic

We're all born under the same sky, but we don't all have the same horizon.

Konrad Adenauer (1876-1967)
German lawyer and statesman

Knowing your destination is half the journey.

Anonymous

Once you say you're going to settle for second, that's what happens to you in life, I find.

John F. Kennedy (1917-1963)
President of United States, 1960-1963

— GOOD —

Do all the good you can,
By all the means you can,
In all the ways you can,
In all the places you can,
At all the times you can,
To all the people you can,
As long as ever you can.

John Wesley (1703-1791)
English evangelist and founder of Methodism

Set your sights high, the higher the better. Expect
the most wonderful things to happen, not in the
future but right now. Realise that nothing is too
good. Allow absolutely nothing to hamper you or
hold you up in any way.

Eileen Caddy
Co-founder of The Findhorn Foundation, Scotland

What is a weed? A plant whose virtues have not been discovered.

Ralph Waldo Emerson (1803-1882)
American poet and essayist

Goodness does not more certainly make men happy than happiness makes them good.

Walter Savage Landor (1775-1864)
English poet and writer

Nothing can harm a good man, either in life or after death.

Socrates (469-399 BC)
Greek philosopher

What is beautiful is good, and who is good will soon also be beautiful.

Sappho (died 610 BC)
Greek lyric poet

— GREATNESS —

There is a great man, who makes every man feel
small. But the real great man is the man who
makes every man feel great.

G.K. Chesterton (1874-1936)
English author

It's great to be great, but it's greater to
be human.

Will Rogers (1879-1935)
American actor and humorist

For the courage of greatness is adventurous and
knows not withdrawing,
But grasps the nettle danger, with resolute hands,
And ever again
Gathers security from the sting of pain.

Vera Brittain (1893-1970)
English author and poet

Lives of great men all remind us
We can make our lives sublime,
And, departing leave behind us
Footprints on the sands of time.

Henry Wadsworth Longfellow (1807-1882)
American poet

We are all worms, but I do believe that I am a
glow-worm.

Sir Winston Churchill (1874-1965)
English statesman

One can build the Empire State Building,
discipline the Prussian army, make a state
hierarchy mightier than God, yet fail to overcome
the unaccountable superiority of certain
human beings.

Alexander Solzhenitsyn (1918-)
Russian writer

— GROWTH —

The great law of culture is: Let each become all
that he was created capable of being.

Thomas Carlyle (1795-1881)
Scottish essayist, historian and philosopher

My business is not to remake myself,
But make the absolute best of what God made.

Robert Browning (1812-1889)
English poet

Love not what you are but what you
may become.

Miguel de Cervantes (1547-1616)
Spanish author

Moments of guilt, moments of contrition,
moments when we are lacking in self-esteem,
moments when we are bearing the trial of being
displeasing to ourselves, are essential to
our growth.

M. Scott Peck (1936-)
American psychiatrist and writer

Be not afraid of growing slowly. Be afraid of
standing still.

Chinese proverb

Examine myself as I may, I can no longer find the
slightest trace of the anxious, agitated individual
of those years, so discontented with herself, so
out of patience with others.

George Sand (Amandine Aurora Lucie Dupin)
(1804-1876)
French novelist

★

Large streams from little fountains flow,
Tall oaks from little acorns grow.

David Everett (1770-1813)
English poet and writer

The creation of a thousand forests is
in one acorn.

Ralph Waldo Emerson (1803-1882)
American essayist, poet and philosopher

Real development is not leaving things behind, as
on a road, but drawing life from them,
as on a root.

G.K. Chesterton (1874-1936)
English writer

ℋ

— HABIT —

Habit is a great deadener.

Samuel Beckett (1906-1989)
Irish novelist and dramatist

The chains of habit are too weak to be felt until
they are too strong to be broken.

Samuel Johnson (1709-1784)
English lexicographer, critic and writer

Habit is habit, and not to be flung out the
window by man, but coaxed downstairs, a
step at a time.

Mark Twain (1835-1910)
American writer and humorist

— HAPPINESS —

One joy scatters a hundred griefs.

Chinese proverb

One is happy as a result of one's own efforts,
once one knows the necessary ingredients of
happiness — simple tastes, a certain degree of
courage, self-denial to a point, love of work, and
above all, a clear conscience. Happiness is no
vague dream.

George Sand (Amandine Aurore Lucie Dupin)
(1804-1876)
French novelist

It is impossible for a man to be made happy by
putting him in a happy place, unless he be first in
a happy state.

Benjamin Whichcote (1609-1683)
English philosopher and theologian

The supreme happiness of life is the conviction that we are loved; loved for ourselves, or rather, loved in spite of ourselves.

Victor Hugo (1802-1885)
French poet and author

Happiness is as a butterfly which, when pursued, is always beyond our grasp, but which, if you will sit down quietly, may alight upon you.

Nathaniel Hawthorne (1804-1864)
American novelist and short story writer

All happiness depends on a leisurely breakfast.

John Gunter (1938-)
English designer

We spend so much time yearning for that special item that will finally make us happy, that we don't take the time to look around and discover that we already are.

Anonymous

Happiness is a mystery like religion, and should
never be rationalised.

G.K. Chesteron (1874-1936)
English author

A lifetime of happiness! No man alive could bear
it: it would be hell on earth.

George Bernard Shaw (1856-1950)
Irish dramatist, essayist and critic

Happiness lies in the joy of achievement and the
thrill of creative effort.

Franklin D. Roosevelt (1882-1945)
President of the United States, 1933-1945

Action may not always bring happiness, but there
is no happiness without action.

Benjamin Disraeli (1804-1881)
English statesman and writer

Knowledge of what is possible is the beginning
of happiness.

George Santayana (1863~1952)
Spanish~American philosopher and poet

Happiness doesn't depend on the actual number
of blessings we manage to scratch from life, only
our attitude towards them.

Alexander Solzhenitsyn (1918~)
Russian writer

When a small child...I thought that success
spelled happiness. I was wrong. Happiness is like
a butterfly which appears and delights us for one
brief moment, but soon flits away.

Anna Pavlova (1881~1931)
Russian ballet dancer

Happiness in this world, when it comes, comes incidentally. Make it the object of pursuit, and it leads us a wild-goose chase, and is never attained.

Nathaniel Hawthorne (1804-1864)
American novelist and short story writer

The happiest people seem to be those who are producing something; the bored people are those who are consuming much and producing nothing.

William Inge (1860-1954)
English prelate and author

To be without some of the things you want is an indispensable part of happiness.

Bertrand Russell (1872-1970)
English philosopher and mathematician

There is no duty we so much underestimate as the duty of being happy. Being happy we sow anonymous benefits upon the world.

Robert Louis Stevenson (1850-1894)
Scottish novelist, poet and essayist

The best way to future happiness is to be as happy as is rightfully possible today.

Charles W. Eliot (1834-1926)
English educator

Most happy is he who is entirely self-reliant, and who centres all his requirements on himself.

Marcus Tullius Cicero (106-43 BC)
Roman orator, statesman and writer

The happiness of life is made up of minute fractions. The little soon forgotten charities of a kiss or smile, a kind look, a hearfelt compliment — countless infinitesimals of pleasurable and genial feelings.

Samuel Taylor Coleridge (1772-1834)
English poet

A man is happy so long as he chooses to
be happy.

Alexander Solzhenitsyn (1918-)
Russian writer

Man's life is happy mainly because he is always
expecting that it will soon be so.

Edgar Allen Poe (1809-1849)
American poet and writer

There is only one happiness in life, to love and to
be loved...

George Sand (Amandine Aurore Lucie Dupin)
(1804-1876)
French novelist

— HATRED —

It's a sign of your own worth sometimes if you
are hated by the right people.

Miles (Stella Maria) Franklin (1879~1954)
Australian writer

Hatred and bitterness can never cure the disease
of fear; only love can do that. Hatred paralyses
life; love harmonises it. Hatred darkens life; love
illumines it.

Martin Luther King (1929~1968)
American black civil-rights leader

Hatred rarely does any harm to its object. It is the
hater who suffers.

Lord Beaverbrook (1879~1964)
Canadian-born newspaper proprietor

— HEALTH —

Health and cheerfulness mutually beget
each other.

Joseph Addison (1672-1719)
English essayist

To wish to be well is a part of becoming well.

Seneca (4 BC-65 AD)
Roman philosopher and statesman

To get the body in tone, get the mind in tune.

Zachary T. Bercovitz (1895-1984)
American doctor and writer

Look to your health; and if you have it, praise
God, and value it next to a good conscience; for
health is the second blessing that we mortals are
capable of; a blessing that money can not buy.

Isaak Walton (1593-1683)
English writer

— HEART —

The heart of the wise, like a mirror, should
reflect all objects, without being sullied by any.

Confucius (551~479 BC)
Chinese philosopher

Keep a green tree in your heart and perhaps a
singing bird will come.

Chinese proverb

The best exercise for the heart is to bend over
backwards for someone else.

Anonymous

I love thee for a heart that's kind.
Not for the knowledge in thy mind.

W.H. Davies (1871~1940)
Welsh poet

— HEAVEN —

Heaven means to be at one with God.

Confucius (551-479 BC)
Chinese philosopher

As much of heaven is visible as we have eyes
to see.

William Winter (1836-1917)
American dramatic critic and poet

The Way of Heaven has no favourites. It is always
with the good man.

Lao-Tze (c.604 BC)
Chinese philosopher and founder of Taoism

Earth has no sorrow that Heaven cannot heal.

Thomas Moore (1779-1852)
Irish poet

— HELP —

If a friend is in trouble, don't annoy him by
asking him if there's anything you can do. Think
of something appropriate and do it.

E.W. Howe (1853-1937)
American writer

No-one is useless in the world who lightens the
burden of it for anyone else.

Charles Dickens (1812-1870)
English author

Many hands make light work.

Proverb

Troubles shared are troubles halved.

Proverb

— HOME —

A man travels the world over in search of what he needs and returns home to find it.

George Moore (1852-1933)
Irish writer and art critic

No place is more delightful than one's own fireside.

Marcus Tullius Cicero (106-43 BC)
Roman orator, statesman and writer

But what on earth is half so dear — so longed for — as the hearth of home?

Emily Brontë (1818-1848)
English poet and novelist

Whom God loves, his house is sweet to him.

Miguel de Cervantes (1547-1616)
Spanish writer

A comfortable home is a great source of happiness. It ranks immediately after health and a good conscience.

Sydney Smith (1771-1845)
English essayist, clergyman and writer

My kitchen is a mystical place, a kind of temple for me. It is a place where the surfaces seem to have significance, where the sounds and odors carry meaning that transfers from the past and bridges to the future.

Pearl Bailey (1918-1986)
American singer

— HONESTY —

Being entirely honest with oneself is a good exercise.

Sigmund Freud (1856-1939)
Austrian founder of psychoanalysis

— HOPE —

There are no hopeless situations; there are only
men who have grown hopeless about them.

Clare Booth Luce (1903-1987)
American playwright

Do not fear to hope...
Each time we smell the autumn's dying scent,
We know that primrose time will come again.

Samuel Taylor Coleridge (1772-1834)
English poet

We should not let our fears hold us back from
pursuing our hopes.

John F. Kennedy (1917-1963)
President of the United States, 1960-1963

Great hopes make great men.

Thomas Fuller (1608-1661)
English divine and historian

We must accept finite disappointment, but we
must never lose infinite hope.

Martin Luther King (1929-1968)
American black civil-rights leader

Hope is itself a species of happiness and, perhaps,
the chief happiness which this world affords.

Samuel Johnson (1709-1784)
English lexicographer, critic and writer

For what human ill does not dawn seem to be
an alleviation?

Thornton Wilder (1897-1975)
American writer

Everything that is done in the world is done
by hope.

Martin Luther (1483-1546)
German religious reformer

– HUMOUR –

Humour is mankind's greatest blessing.

Mark Twain (1835-1910)
American writer and humorist

Total absence of humour renders life impossible.

Colette (1873-1954)
French novelist

Everything is funny, as long as it's happening to
somebody else.

Will Rogers (1879-1935)
American actor and humorist

He deserves paradise who makes his
companions laugh.

The Koran

I

— IDEAS —

Greater than the tread of mighty armies is an idea whose time has come.

Victor Hugo (1802-1885)
French poet and author

A crank is a man with a new idea — until it catches on.

Mark Twain (1835-1910)
American writer and humorist

What was once thought can never be unthought.

Friedrich Durrenmatt (1921-)
Swiss writer

If you don't follow through on your creative ideas, someone else will pick them up and use them. When you get an idea of this sort, you should jump in with both feet, not just stick your toe in the water... Be daring, be fearless, and don't be afraid that somebody is going to criticize you or laugh at you. If your ego is not involved no-one can hurt you.

Guru RHH

A stand can be made against invasion by an army; no stand can be made against invasion by an idea.

Victor Hugo (1802-1885)
French writer

— IGNORANCE —

To be conscious that you are ignorant is a great step to knowledge.

Benjamin Disraeli (1804-1881)
English statesman and writer

— IMAGINATION —

What is now proved was once only imagined.

William Blake (1757-1827)
English poet, artist and mystic

Man's mind, once stretched by a new idea, never
regains its original dimension.

Oliver Wendell Holmes (1809-1894)
American writer

Imagination is more important than knowledge.

Albert Einstein (1879-1955)
German-born physicist

This world is but canvas to our imaginations.

Henry David Thoreau (1817-1862)
American essayist, poet and mystic

Imagination is the highest kite one can fly.

Lauren Bacall (1924-)
American actress

Imagination, industry and intelligence — 'the three I's' — are all indispensable to the actress, but of these three the greatest is, without any doubt, imagination.

Ellen Terry (1848-1928)
English actress

There are no rules of architecture for a castle in the clouds.

G.K. Chesterton (1874-1936)
English critic, novelist and poet

— IMPERFECTION —

No one should abandon duties because he see defects in them. Every action, every activity, is surrounded by defects as a fire is surrounded by smoke.

Bhagavad Gita

— IMPRESSION —

You never get a second chance to make a good first impression.

Anonymous

Every man is a hero and an oracle to somebody, and to that person, whatever he says has an enhanced value.

Ralph Waldo Emerson (1803-1882)
American essayist, poet and philosopher

— INDEPENDENCE —

Depend not on another, but lean instead on thyself...True happiness is born of self-reliance.

The Laws of Manu, Hindu teachings

It's easy to be independent when you've got money. But to be independent when you haven't got a thing — that's the Lord's test.

Mahalia Jackson (1911-1972)
American spirituals singer

The strongest man in the world is he who stands alone.

Henrik Ibsen (1828-1906)
Norwegian dramatist

Follow your own bent, no matter what people say.

Karl Marx (1818-1883)
German philosopher

— INDIVIDUALITY —

Conformity is one of the most fundamental dishonesties of all. When we reject our specialness, water down our God-given individuality and uniqueness, we begin to lose our freedom. The conformist is in no way a free man. He has to follow the herd.

Norman Vincent Peale (1898-1993)
American writer and minister

Every individual has a place to fill in the world, and is important, in some respect, whether he chooses to be or not.

Nathaniel Hawthorne (1804-1864)
American novelist

— INTEGRITY —

If you don't stand for something...you'll fall
for anything.

Anonymous

Integrity without knowledge is weak and useless,
and knowledge without integrity is dangerous
and dreadful.

Samuel Johnson (1709~1784)
British lexicographer, critic and writer

My strength is as the strength of ten,
Because my heart is pure.

Alfred, Lord Tennyson (1809~1892)
English poet

This above all — to thine own self be true,
And it must follow, as night follows day,
Thou canst not then be false to any man.

William Shakespeare (1564~1616)
English playwright and poet

— *INTUITION* —

Intelligence highly awakened is intuition, which
is the only true guide in life.

Jiddu Krishnamurti (1895-1986)
Indian theosophist

We belittle an intuition, calling it only a hunch,
and therefore not be taken too seriously. I
encourage you to take your hunches and
intuitions very seriously. They contain some of
your highest, most profound insights
and wisdom.

Lucia Capacchione
American art therapist and pioneer in inner healing

Intuition is a truth that arrives in the
mind unbidden.

Anonymous

J

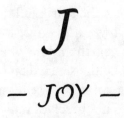

– JOY –

May your joys be as deep as the ocean, your
sorrows as light as its foam.

Anonymous

The life without festivals is a long road without
an inn.

Democritus (c.460 BC)
Greek philosopher

Joy exists only in self-acceptance. Seek perfect
acceptance, not a perfect life.

Anonymous

Joy is not in things; it is in us.

Richard Wagner (1813-1883)
German composer

Joy, Lady, is the spirit and the power,
Which wedding nature gives to us in dower,
A new earth and new heaven,
Undreamt of by the sensual and the proud —
Joy is the sweet voice, joy the luminous cloud —
We in ourselves rejoice.

Samuel Taylor Coleridge (1772-1834)
English poet

Joy is one of nature's greatest medicines. Joy is always healthy. A pleasant state of mind tends to bring abnormal conditions back to normal.

Catherine Ponder
American motivational writer

Taking joy in life is a woman's best cosmetic.

Rosalind Russell (1911-1976)
American actress

The more joy we have, the more nearly perfect we are.

Benedict Spinoza (1632-1677)
Dutch philosopher

— JUDGEMENT —

Each person you meet is in a specific stage of
their life, a stage you may have passed or not yet
reached. Judging them by your standards and
experience is therefore not only unfair, but could
lead to unnecessary anger and frustration.

Anonymous

— JUSTICE —

Though the sword of justice is sharp, it will not
slay the innocent.

Chinese proverb

Justice is truth in action.

Benjamin Disraeli (1804-1881)
English statesman and writer

K

— KINDNESS —

Recompense injury with justice, and recompense
kindness with kindness.

Confucius (551~479 BC)
Chinese philosopher

No act of kindness, no matter how small, is
ever wasted.

Aesop (c. 550 BC)
Greek fable-maker

My religion is very simple — my religion
is kindness.

Dalai Lama (1935-)
Tibetan spiritual leader

Kindness is a language which the blind can see
and the deaf can hear.

Anonymous

Think deeply; speak gently; love much; laugh
often; work hard; give freely; pay promptly;
be kind.

Anonymous

I expect to pass through life but once. If,
therefore, there be any kindness I can show, or
any good thing I can do to any fellow being, let
me do it now, for I shall not pass this way again.

William Penn (1644-1718)
English Quaker and founder of Pennsylvania, USA

Little deeds of kindness,
Little words of love,
Help to make earth happy
Like the heaven above.

Julia Fletcher Carney (1823-1908)
American teacher

We cannot always return an act of kindness to
the person who bestowed it, but we can pay back
the debt by helping others.

Anonymous

Wise words often fall on barren ground; but a
kind word is never thrown away.

Arthur Helps (1813-1875)
English historian

Kindness which is bestowed on the good
is never lost.

Plato (426-c.347 BC)
Greek philosopher

The heart benevolent and kind
The most resembles God.

Robert Burns (1759-1796)
Scottish poet

The best portion of a good man's life,
His little, nameless, unremembered acts of
kindness and love.

William Wordsworth (1770-1850)
English poet

Getting money is not all a man's business: to
cultivate kindness is a valuable part of the
business of life.

Samuel Johnson (1709-1784)
English lexicographer, critic and writer

One kind word can warm three winter months.

Japanese saying

— KNOWLEDGE —

I thank Thee, Lord, for knowing me better than I
know myself,
And for letting me know myself better than
others know me.
I pray Thee then, make me better than they
suppose,
And forgive me for what they do not know.

Abu Bekr (573-634)
Father-in-law of Mohammed, his follower and successor

We do not know one-millionth of one per cent
about anything.

Thomas A. Edison (1847-1931)
American inventor

I am sufficiently proud of my knowing
something to be modest about my not knowing
everything.

Vladimir Nabokov (1899-1977)
Russian-born American author

A good listener is not only popular everywhere,
but after a while he gets to know something.

Wilson Mizner (1876-1933)
American humorist

Knowledge and timber shouldn't be much used
till they are seasoned.

Oliver Wendell Holmes (1809-1894)
American writer and physician

Knowledge is the action of the soul.

Ben Jonson (1573-1637)
English dramatist

Knowledge advances by steps, and not by leaps.

Thomas Macaulay (1800-1859)
English historian and statesman

An investment in knowledge always pays the best interest.

Benjamin Franklin (1706-1790)
American statesman and philosopher

What we want is to see the child in pursuit of knowledge, and not knowledge in pursuit of the child.

George Bernard Shaw (1856-1950)
Irish dramatist, essayist and critic

It is the greatest nuisance that knowledge can only be acquired by hard work.

W. Somerset Maugham (1874-1965)
English writer

Knowledge is power.

Francis Bacon (1561-1626)
English philosopher

L

— LAUGHTER —

Laughter is the sensation of feeling good all over, and showing it principally in one place.

Josh Billings (1818-1885)
American humorist

Laughter is sunshine in a house.

William Makepeace Thackeray (1811-1863)
English author

A complete revaluation takes place in your physical and mental being when you've laughed and had some fun.

Catherine Ponder
American motivational writer

Laughter has something in it in common with the
ancient winds of faith and inspiration; it
unfreezes pride and unwinds secrecy; it makes
men forget themselves in the presence of
something greater than themselves; something
that they cannot resist.

G.K. Chesterton (1874-1936)
English critic, novelist and poet

The most wasted of all days is that on which one
has not laughed.

Nicolas Chamfort (1741-94)
French writer

Laugh and the world laughs with you;
Weep, and you weep alone.

Ella Wheeler Wilcox (1850-1919)
American poet

It's impossible to speak highly enough of the
virtues, the dangers and the power of
shared laughter.

Françoise Sagan (1935-)
French novelist

We are all here for a spell. Get all the good
laughs you can.

Will Rogers (1879-1935)
American actor and humorist

Among those whom I like or admire, I can find
no common denominator, but among those I love,
I can: all of them make me laugh.

W.H. Auden (1907-1973)
English poet and essayist

He who laughs, lasts.

Anonymous

— LAZINESS —

For one person who dreams of making fifty
thousand pounds, a hundred people dream of
being left fifty thousand pounds.

A.A. Milne (1882-1956)
English writer

It is the doom of laziness and gluttony to be
inactive without ease, and drowsy
without tranquillity.

Samuel Johnson (1709-1784)
English lexicographer, critic and writer

Indolence is a delightful but distressing state. We
must be doing something to be happy.

William Hazlitt (1778-1830)
English essayist

— LEADERSHIP —

I learned that a great leader is a man who has the ability to get other people to do what they don't want to do and like it.

Harry S. Truman (1884-1972)
President of the United States, 1945-1952

Leadership: the art of getting someone else to do something you want done because he wants to do it.

Dwight D. Eisenhower (1890-1969)
President of the United States, 1953-1961

The great difference between the real leader and the pretender is — that the one sees into the future, while the other regards only the present; the one lives by the day, and acts upon expediency; the other acts on enduring principles and for immortality.

Edmund Burke (1729-1797)
British politician and writer

— LEARNING —

Blessed are those who listen, for they shall learn.

Anonymous

No man e'er found a happy life by chance,
Or yawned it into being with a wish.
An art it is, and must be learnt; and learnt
With unremitting effort, or be lost.

Edward Young (1683-1765)
English poet

Have you learned lessons only of those who
admired you, and were tender with you, and
stood aside for you? Have you not learned great
lessons from those who braced themselves
against you, and disputed the passage with you?

Walt Whitman (1819-1891)
American poet

That is what learning is. You suddenly understand something you've understood all your life, but in a new way.

Doris Lessing (1919-)
English novelist

What we have to learn to do, we learn by doing.

Aristotle (384-322 BC)
Greek philosopher

Natural abilities are like natural plants; they need pruning by study.

Francis Bacon (1561-1626)
English philosopher

Learning makes a man fit company for himself.

Thomas Fuller (1608-1661)
English divine and historian

— LIFE —

To live long, live slowly.

Marcus Tullius Cicero (106-43 BC)
Roman orator, statesman and writer

Decide carefully, exactly what you want in life,
then work like mad to make sure you get it!

Hector Crawford (1913-1991)
Australian television program-maker

Life is either a daring adventure or nothing.

Helen Keller (1880-1968)
Deaf and blind American lecturer, writer and scholar.

Live every day as though it's your last. One day
you'll get it right!

Zig Ziglar
American writer and motivational speaker

Life is what happens to you while you're busy making other plans.

John Lennon (1940-1980)
English singer and songwriter

When I hear somebody sigh, 'Life is hard,' I am always tempted to ask, 'Compared to what?'

Sydney J. Harris (1917-)
Newspaper columnist

The greatest use of life is to spend it for something that will outlast it.

William James (1842-1910)
American psychologist and philosopher

Life begets life. Energy creates energy. It is by spending oneself that one becomes rich.

Sarah Bernhardt (1844-1923)
French actress

Each player must accept the cards life deals him.
But once they are in hand, he alone must decide
how to play the cards in order to win the game.

Voltaire (1694-1778)
French author

Life is not the way it's supposed to be. It's the way
it is. The way you cope with it is what makes the
difference.

Anonymous

I have a simple philosophy. Fill what's empty.
Empty what's full. And scratch where it itches.

Alice Roosevelt Longworth (1884-1980)
Daughter of American President Theodore Roosevelt

The first rule in opera is the first rule in life: see
to everything yourself.

Dame Nellie Melba (1865-1931)
Australian opera singer

There is no cure for birth and death, save to enjoy the interval.

George Santayana (1863-1952)
Spanish-American philosopher and poet

The main fact of life for me is love or its absence. Whether life is worth living depends on whether there is love in life.

R.D. Laing (1927-)
Scottish psychiatrist

You must understand the whole of life, not just one little part of it. That is why you must read, that is why you must look at the skies, that is why you must sing and dance, and write poems, and suffer; and understand, for all that is life.

Jiddu Krishnamurti (1895-1986)
Indian theosophist

When you were born, you cried and the world rejoiced. Live your life in such a manner that when you die the world cries and you rejoice.

Traditional Indian saying

Life can only be understood backwards; but it must be lived forwards.

Soren Aaby Kierkegaard (1813-1855)
Danish philosopher and theologian

Live all you can; it's a mistake not to. It doesn't so much matter what you do in particular, so long as you have had your life. If you haven't had that, what have you had?

Henry James (1843-1916)
American novelist

These, then, are my last words to you: be not afraid of life. Believe that life is worth living, and your belief will help create the fact.

William James (1842-1910)
American psychologist and philosopher

✦

We love life; not because we are used to living,
but because we are used to loving.

Friedrich Wilhelm Nietzsche (1844-1900)
German philosopher, poet and scholar

The more we live by our intellect, the less we
understand the meaning of life.

Leo Tolstoy (1828-1910)
Russian writer

Children FEEL life. They smell it, roll in it, run
with it, see it all around them. Feel the world
through the eyes of a child.

Anonymous

Life is not made up of great sacrifices and duties
but of little things: in which smiles and kindness
given habitually are what win and preserve the
heart and secure comfort.

Sir Humphry Davy (1778-1829)
English chemist and poet

I want to be thoroughly used up when I die...Life is no brief candle to me. It's a sort of splendid torch which I've got to hold up for the moment and I want to make it burn as brightly as possible before handing it on to future generations.

George Bernard Shaw (1856-1950)
Irish dramatist, essayist and critic

I like life. I have sometimes been wildly, despairingly, acutely miserable, racked with sorrow, but through it all I still know quite certainly that just to be alive is a grand thing.

Agatha Christie (1890-1976)
English mystery writer

Life was meant to be lived. Curiosity must be kept alive...One must never, for whatever reason, turn his back on life.

Eleanor Roosevelt (1884-1962)
First Lady of the United States, 1933-1945

— *LONELINESS* —

Pray that your loneliness may spur you into finding something to live for, great enough to die for.

Dag Hammerskjold (1905-1961)
Swedish diplomat

No man is lonely while eating a bowl of spaghetti.

Sign in a spaghetti bar

That is part of the beauty of all literature. You discover that your longings are universal longings, that you're not lonely and isolated from anyone. You belong.

F. Scott Fitzgerald (1896-1940)
American novelist

— LOVE —

The rule for us all is perfectly simple. Do not waste time bothering whether you 'love' your neighbour; act as if you did. As soon as we do this we find one of the great secrets. When you are behaving as if you loved someone, you will presently come to love him.

C.S. Lewis (1898-1963)
Irish-born academic, writer and poet

The only thing I know about love is that love is all there is...Love can do all but raise the dead.

Emily Dickinson (1830-1886)
American poet

Let us not be satisfied with just giving money. Money is not enough, money can be got, but they need your hearts to love them. So, spread love everywhere you go: first of all in your own home. Give love to your children, to your wife or husband, to a next-door neighbour.

Mother Teresa of Calcutta (1910-)
Yugoslav-born missionary

To love means never to be afraid of the windstorms of life: should you shield the canyons from the windstorms you would never see the true beauty of their carvings.

Elisabeth Kubler-Ross (1926-)
Swiss-born American psychiatrist

Him that I love, I wish to be free — even from me.

Anne Morrow Lindbergh (1906-)
American writer and aviator

Love is a fruit in season at all times, and within the reach of every hand. Anyone may gather it and no limit is set. Everyone can reach this love through meditation, spirit of prayer, and sacrifice, by an intense inner life.

Mother Teresa of Calcutta (1910-)
Yugoslav-born missionary

Love means to commit oneself without guarantee, to give oneself completely in the hope that our love will produce love in the loved person. Love is an act of faith, and whoever is of little faith is of little love.

Erich Fromm (1900-1980)
German-American psychoanalyst

I will greet this day with love in my heart. And how will I do this? Henceforth will I look on all things with love and I will be born again. I will love the sun for it warms my bones; yet I will love the rain for it cleanses my spirit. I will love the light for it shows me the way; yet I will love the darkness for it shows me the stars. I will welcome happiness for it enlarges my heart; yet I will endure sadness for it opens my soul. I will ac-knowledge rewards for they are my due; yet I will welcome obstacles for they are my challenge.

Og Mandino (1923-)
American author

Love seems the swiftest, but it is the slowest of all growths. No man or woman really knows what perfect love is until they have been married for a quarter of a century.

Mark Twain (1835-1910)
American writer and humorist

Love is like quicksilver in the hand.
Leave the fingers open and it stays.
Clutch it, and it darts away.

Dorothy Parker (1893-1967)
American writer and satirist

Love consists in this, that two solitudes protect and touch and greet each other.

Rainer Maria Rilke (1875-1926)
Austrian poet

Love is, above all, the gift of oneself.

Jean Anouilh (1910-1987)
French dramatist

Love does not consist in gazing at each other but in looking together in the same direction.

Antoine de Saint-Exupery (1900-1944)
French airman and author

By love serve one another.

Galatians 5:13

Treasure the love you receive above all. It will survive long after your gold and good health have vanished.

Og Mandino (1923-)
American author

Men and women are made to love each other. It's only by loving each other that they can achieve anything.

Christina Stead (1902-1983)
Australian writer

I know of only one duty, and that is to love.

Albert Camus (1913-1960)
French writer

God doesn't look at how much we do, but with how much love we do it.

Mother Teresa of Calcutta (1910-)
Yugoslav-born missionary

Love is the free exercise of choice. Two people love each other only when they are quite capable of living without each other but choose to live with each other.

M. Scott Peck (1936-)
American psychiatrist and writer

The heart has reasons which the reason
cannot understand.

Blaise Pascal (1623-1662)
French physicist, theologian and writer

Love gives naught but itself and takes naught but
from itself. Love possesses not nor would it be
possessed; for love is sufficient unto love.

Khalil Gibran (1883-1931)
Lebanese poet, writer, artist and mystic

I define love thus: the will to extend oneself for
the purpose of nurturing one's own or another's
spiritual growth.

M. Scott Peck (1936-)
American psychiatrist and writer

— LUCK —

Anyone who does not know how to make the
most of his luck has no right to complain if it
passes him by.

Miguel de Cervantes (1547-1616)
Spanish author

I am a great believer in luck, and I find the
harder I work the more I have of it.

Stephen Leacock (1869-1944)
English-born Canadian economist and humorist

Luck to me is something else. Hard work — and
realising what is opportunity and what isn't.

Lucille Ball (1911-1989)
American actress

M

— MARRIAGE —

A happy marriage has in it all the pleasures of a friendship, all the enjoyments of sense and reason, and indeed, all the sweets of life.

Joseph Addison (1672-1719)
English essayist and politician

There is no more lovely, friendly, and charming relationship, communion, or company than a good marriage.

Martin Luther (1483-1544)
German religious reformer

Let there be spaces in your togetherness.

Kahlil Gibran (1883-1931)
Lebanese poet, writer, artist and mystic

Chains do not hold a marriage together. It is threads, hundreds of tiny threads which sew people together through the years. That is what makes a marriage last — more than passion or even sex.

Simone Signoret (1921-1985)
French actress

Give your hearts, but not into each
other's keeping,
For only the hand of life can contain your hearts.
And stand together yet not too near together:
For the pillars of the temple stand apart,
And the oak tree and the cypress grow not in
each other's shadow.

Kahlil Gibran (1883-1931)
Lebanese poet, artist and mystic

Two things do prolong thy life.
A quiet heart and a loving wife.

Anonymous

— MIND —

One man who has a mind and knows it can always beat ten men who haven't and don't.

George Bernard Shaw (1856-1950)
Irish dramatist, essayist and critic

Luck favours the mind that is prepared.

Louis Pasteur (1822-1895)
French bacteriologist

When people will not weed their own minds, they are apt to be overrun with nettles.

Horace Walpole (1717-1797)
English writer

The mind of man is capable of anything — because everything is in it, all the past as well as the future.

Joseph Conrad (1857-1924)
English novelist

The greater part of our happiness or misery depends on our dispositions and not on our circumstances. We carry the seeds of the one or the other about with us in our minds wherever we go.

Martha Washington (1731-1802)
First Lady of the United States, 1789-1799

The mind is its own place, and in itself
Can make a heaven of hell, a hell of heaven.

John Milton (1606-1674)
English poet

— MIRACLES —

Miracles happen to those who believe in them.

Bernhard Berenson (1865-1959)
American art critic

The miracle is not to fly in the air, or to walk on
the water; but to walk on the earth.

Chinese proverb

Where there is great love, there are
always miracles.

Willa Cather (1873-1947)
American writer

A miracle is an event which creates faith. Frauds
deceive. An event which creates faith does not
deceive; therefore it is not a fraud, but a miracle.

George Bernard Shaw (1856-1950)
Irish dramatist, playwright and critic

Everything is miraculous. It is a miracle that one does not melt in one's bath.

Pablo Picasso (1881-1973)
Spanish painter

Why, who makes much of a miracle?
As to me I known nothing else but miracles —
To me every hour of night and day is a miracle,
Every cubic inch of space a miracle.

Walt Whitman (1819-1891)
American poet

The miracles of nature are all around us.

Anonymous

— MISERY —

Human misery must somewhere have a stop;
There is no wind that always blows a storm.

Euripides (480-406 BC)
Greek dramatist

The secret of being miserable is to have leisure to
bother about whether you are happy or not.

George Bernard Shaw (1856-1950)
Irish dramatist and critic

One often calms one's grief by recounting it.

Pierre Cornelle (1606-1684)
French dramatist

Who going through the vale of misery use it for a
well; and the pools are filled with water. They go
from strength to strength.

Psalm 84:6-7

— MISTAKES —

I have learned more from my mistakes than from my successes.

Sir Humphry Davy (1778-1829)
English chemist and poet

Nothing would be done at all if a man waited until he could do it so well that no-one could find fault with it.

Cardinal John Henry Newman (1801-1890)
English theologian

The greatest mistake you can make in life is to be continually fearing you will make one.

Elbert Hubbard (1856-1915)
American writer

There's nothing wrong in making a mistake — as long as you don't follow it up with encores.

Anonymous

It is the greatest of all mistakes to do nothing
because you can only do little.

Sydney Smith (1771-1845)
English essayist, clergyman and wit

It has taken me thirty-three years and a bang on
the head to get my values right.

Stirling Moss (1929-)
English racing driver

If you have made mistakes...there is always
another chance for you...you may have a fresh
start any moment you choose, for this thing we
call 'failure' is not the falling down, but the
staying down.

Mary Pickford (1893-1979)
American actress

Some of the best lessons we ever learn, we learn
from our mistakes and failures. The error of the
past is the success and wisdom of the future.

Tyron Edwards (1809-1894)
American theologian

He who never made a mistake never made
a discovery.

Samuel Smiles (1812~1904)
Scottish author and social reformer

The man who makes no mistakes does not
usually make anything.

Edward John Phelps (1822~1900)
American lawyer and diplomat

A man should never be ashamed to own he has
been in the wrong, which is but saying, in other
words, that he is wiser today than he
was yesterday.

Alexander Pope (1688~1744)
English poet

Every great mistake has a halfway moment, a split second when it can be recalled and perhaps remedied.

Pearl S. Buck (1892~1973)
American writer

There are no mistakes, no coincidences; all events are blessings given to us to learn from. There is no need to go to India or anywhere else to find peace. You will find that deep place of silence right in your room, your garden or even your bathtub.

Elisabeth Kubler-Ross (1926~)
Swiss-born American psychiatrist

A life spent making mistakes is not only more honourable but more useful than a life spent doing nothing.

George Bernard Shaw (1856~1950)
Irish dramatist, essayist and critic

— MONEY —

The shortest and best way to make your fortune
is to let people see clearly that it is in their
interests to promote yours.

Jean de la Bruyere (1645-1696)
French satirist

Money, it turned out, was exactly like sex: you
thought of nothing else if you didn't have it and
thought of other things if you did.

James Baldwin (1924-1987)
American writer

Money is like an arm or leg — use it or lose it.

Henry Ford (1863-1947)
American motor car manufacturer

Money can't buy friends, but you can get a better
class of enemy.

Spike Milligan (1918-)
English comedian

If money is your hope for independence you will never have it. The only real security that a man can have in this world is a reserve of knowledge, experience and ability.

Henry Ford (1863-1947)
American motor car manufacturer

Money makes money, and the money money makes, makes more money.

Benjamin Franklin (1706-1790)
American statesman and philosopher

Money is like muck, not good except to be spread.

Francis Bacon (1561-1626)
English philosopher

— MUSIC —

I think I should have no other mortal wants, if I could always have plenty of music. It seems to infuse strength into my limbs and ideas into my brain. Life seems to go on without effort, when I am filled with music.

George Eliot (Mary Ann Evans) (1819-1880)
English novelist

Music is the medicine of the troubled mind.

Walter Haddon (1516-1537)
English writer

He who hears music feels his solitude peopled at once.

Robert Browning (1812-1889)
English poet

N

— NATURE —

There can be no very black misery to him who lives in the midst of Nature and has his senses still.

Henry David Thoreau (1817-1862)
American essayist, poet and mystic

Every part of this Earth is sacred to my people. Every shining pine needle, every sandy shore, every mist in the dark woods, every clearing and humming insect is holy in the memory and experience of my people

Chief Seathl
From a letter written in 1883 to the President of the United States.

— NEGATIVITY —

Every day is irreplaceable, so don't ruin yours by allowing the negative moods of others to pull you into their frame of mind.

Anonymous

Try to avoid pessimists — negativity can be catching.

Anonymous

Don't be too self-critical. Learn to be on your own side.

Anonymous

— NEGOTIATION —

Let us never negotiate out of fear, but let us never fear to negotiate.

John F. Kennedy (1917-1963)
President of the United States, 1961-1963

O

— OCCUPATION —

When men are rightly occupied, then
amusement grows out of the work as the
colour-petals out of a fruitful flower; when they
are faithfully helpful and compassionate, all their
emotions become steady, deep, perpetual and
vivifying to the soul as the natural
pulse to the body.

John Ruskin (1819-1900)
English author and art critic

Good for the body is the work of the body, good
for the soul is the work of the soul, and good for
either the work of the other.

Henry David Thoreau (1817-1862)
American essayist, poet and mystic

— OPPORTUNITY —

One cannot step twice into the same river.

Heraclitus (c.540-c.480 BC)
Greek philosopher

Problems are only opportunities in work clothes.

Henry John Kaiser (1882-1967)
American industrialist

A wise man will make more opportunities than
he finds.

Francis Bacon (1561-1626)
English philosopher

Do not wait for extraordinary circumstances to
do good; try to use ordinary situations.

Jean Paul Richter (1763-1825)
German novelist and humorist

Failure is only the opportunity to begin again more intelligently.

Henry Ford (1863-1947)
American motor car manufacturer

★

If heaven drops a date, open your mouth.

Chinese proverb

★

In the middle of difficulty lies opportunity.

Albert Einstein (1879-1955)
German-born physicist

★

A diamond is a chunk of coal that made good under pressure.

Anonymous

To improve the golden moment of opportunity, and catch the good that is within our reach, is the great art of life.

William James (1842-1910)
American psychologist and philosopher

Opportunities are usually disguised as hard work, so most people don't recognise them.

Ann Landers (1918-)
American journalist

The people who get on in this world are the people who get up and look for the circumstances they want, and, if they can't find them, make them.

George Bernard Shaw (1856-1950)
Irish dramatist, essayist and critic

— OPTIMISM —

When one door shuts, another opens.

Proverb

In the midst of winter, I finally learned there was
in me an invincible summer.

Albert Camus (1913-1960)
French writer

An optimist is a person who takes action, who
moves out ahead of the crowd.

Anonymous

The optimist proclaims we live in the best of all
possible worlds; and the pessimist fears this
is true.

James Cabell (1879-1958)
American novelist and journalist

No pessimist ever discovered the secrets of the stars, or sailed to an uncharted land, or opened a new heaven to the horizon of the spirit.

Helen Keller (1880-1968)
Deaf and blind American lecturer, writer and scholar

I count only the sunny hours.

Sundial inscription

As you make your way through life,
Let this ever be your goal,
Keep your eye upon the doughnut
And not upon the hole.

Anonymous

A pessimist sees a glass that's half empty. An optimist sees a glass that's half full.

Anonymous

Over the winter glaciers
I see the summer glow;
And through the wild-piled snowdrift
The warm rosebuds below.

Ralph Waldo Emerson (1803-1882)
American essayist, poet and philosopher

To look up and not down,
To look forward and not back,
To look out and not in —
To lend a hand!

Edward Everett Hale (1882-1909)
American Unitarian clergyman and inspirational writer

An optimist sees an opportunity in every
calamity. A pessimist sees a calamity in
every opportunity.

Anonymous

— ORDER —

Order is the sanity of the mind, the health of the
body, the peace of the city, the serenity
of the state.

Chinese proverb

As the beams to a house, as the bones to the body
— so is order to all things.

Robert Southey (1774-1843)
English poet

Order is heaven's first law.

Alexander Pope (1688-1744)
English poet

A place for everything, and everything in
its place.

Samuel Smiles (1812-1904)
Scottish author and social reformer

— ORGANISATION —

Organisation is always the cornerstone of
business success.

Anonymous

A well-spent day brings happy sleep.

Leonardo da Vinci (1452-1519)
Italian painter, sculptor, architect and inventor

I must create a system, or be enslaved by
another man's.

William Blake (1757-1827)
English poet

Let all things be done decently and in order.

Corinthians 14:40

— ORIGINALITY —

What is originality? It is being one's self, and
reporting accurately what we see.

Ralph Waldo Emerson (1803-1882)
American essayist, poet and philosopher

All good things which exist are the fruits
of originality.

John Stuart Mill (1806-1873)
English philosopher

The dogmas of the quiet past are inadequate to
the stormy present. The occasion is piled high
with difficulty, and we must rise to the occasion.
As our case is new, so must we think anew and
act anew.

Abraham Lincoln (1809-1865)
President of the United States, 1860-1863

P

— PAIN —

The best way out of emotional pain is through it.

Anonymous

— PARTING —

Moments of kindness and reconciliation are
worth having, even if the parting has to come
sooner or later.

Alice Munro (1931~)
American writer

Weep if you must,
Parting is here —
But life goes on,
So sing as well.

Joyce Grenfell (1910-1979)
English comedian and writer

— PARENTHOOD —

Who of us is mature enough for offspring before
the offspring themselves arrive? The value of
marriage is not that adults produce children but
that children produce adults.

Peter de Vries (1910-)
American novelist

Children are a bridge to heaven.

Anonymous

A mother is not a person to lean on but a person
to make leaning unnecessary.

Dorothy Canfield Fisher (1879-1958)
American writer

One mother teaches more than a
hundred teachers.

Jewish proverb

Love children especially, for, like angels, they too are sinless, and they live to soften and purify our hearts and, as it were, to guide us.

Feodor Dostoevsky (1821-1881)
Russian writer

Always believe in yourselves as parents. You are the best your children have.

Anonymous

Anything that parents have not learned from experience they can now learn from their children.

Anonymous

Children are likely to live up to what you believe of them.

Lady Bird Johnson (1912-)
First Lady of the United States, 1963-1969

— PAST —

The past exists only in memory, consequences,
effects. It has power over me only as I give it my
power. I can let go, release it, move freely, I am
not my past.

Anonymous

Even God cannot change the past.

Agathon (c. 446-401 BC)
Greek poet and playwright

Study the past, if you would divine the future.

Confucius (551-479 BC)
Chinese philosopher

— PATIENCE —

With time and patience the mulberry leaf
becomes a silk gown.

Chinese saying

Never cut what you can untie.

Joseph Joubert (1754-1824)
French writer

Patience is a bitter plant, but it has sweet fruit.

Proverb

There is nothing so bitter that a patient mind
cannot find some solace in it.

Lucius Annaeus Seneca (c.55 BC-c.40 AD)
Roman rhetorician

— PEACE —

Deep peace of the running wave to you.
Deep peace of the flowing air to you.
Deep peace of the quiet earth to you.
Deep peace of the shining stars to you.
Deep peace of the Son of Peace to you.

Celtic benediction

Do not be in a hurry to fill up an empty space
with words and embellishments, before it has
been filled with a deep interior peace.

Father Alexander Elchaninov
Russian priest

Do not lose your inward peace for anything
whatsoever, even if your whole world
seems upset.

Saint Francis de Sales (1567-1622)
French Roman Catholic bishop and writer

You will give yourself peace of mind if you perform every act of your life as if it were
your last.

Marcus Aurelius (121-180 AD)
Roman emperor and philosopher

Find peace within yourself by accepting not only
what you are, but what you are never
going to be.

Anonymous

Under this tree, where light and shade
Speckle the grass like a Thrush's breast,
Here in this green and quiet place
I give myself to peace and rest.
The peace of my contented mind,
That is to me a wealth untold —
When the Moon has no more silver left,
And the Sun's at the end of his gold.

W.H. Davies (1870-1940)
Welsh poet

— PERCEPTION —

If the doors of perception were cleansed,
everything would appear to man as it is, infinite.
For man has closed himself up, till he sees all
things through narrow chinks of his cavern.

William Blake (1757-1827)
English poet, artist and mystic

— PERSEVERANCE —

The drops of rain make a hole in the stone not by
violence but by oft falling.

Lucretius (96-55 BC)
Roman poet

God helps those who persevere.

The Koran

But what if I fail of my purpose here?
It is but to keep the nerves at strain,
To dry one's eyes and laugh at a fall,
And, baffled, get up and begin again.

Robert Browning (1812-1889)
English poet

Step by step the ladder is ascended.

George Herbert (1593-1633)
English poet

Consider the postage stamp; its usefulness
consists in the ability to stick to one thing
till it gets there.

Josh Billings (1818-1885)
American humorist

Finish whatever you begin, and experience the
triumph of completion.

Anonymous

Nothing in the world can take the place of persistence. Talent will not; nothing is more common than unsuccessful men with talent. Genius will not; unrewarded genius is almost a proverb. Education will not; the world is full of educated failures. Persistence and determination alone are omnipotent.

Calvin Coolidge (1872-1933)
President of the United States 1923-1929

To keep a lamp burning we have to keep putting oil in it.

Mother Teresa of Calcutta (1910-)
Yugoslav-born missionary

I have learned that success is to be measured not so much by the position one has reached in life as by the obstacles which one has overcome while trying to succeed.

Brooker T. Washington (1856-1915)
American black reformer

— PICK-ME-UPS —

It is almost impossible to remember how tragic a place the world is when one is playing golf.

Robert Lynd (1879-1949)
Irish essayist and journalist

There are a few things a hot bath won't cure, but I don't known many of them.

Sylvia Plath (1932-1963)
American poet and writer

Noble deeds and hot baths are the best cures for depression.

Dodie Smith (1896-1990)
English Writer

Where's the man could ease the heart
Like a satin gown?

Dorothy Parker (1893-1967)
American writer and satirist

Thank God for tea. What would the world do
without tea?

Sydney Smith (1771-1845)
English clergyman and essayist

Drink tea and forget the world's noises.

Chinese saying

A walk at dawn works wonders for the soul.

Anonymous

A little of what you fancy does you good.

English music hall song

— PLAN —

Plan your work and work your plan.

Norman Vincent Peale (1898-1993)
American writer and minister

Plan for the future because that's where you are
going to spend the rest of your life.

Mark Twain (1835-1910)
American writer and humorist

The time to repair the roof is when the sun
is shining.

John F. Kennedy (1917-1963)
President of the United States, 1961-1963

— PLEASURE —

One ought every day at least to hear a little song, read a good poem, see a fine picture, and, if it were possible, to speak a few reasonable words.

Johann Wolfgang von Goethe (1749-1832)
German poet, novelist and playwright

Life affords no higher pleasure than that of surmounting difficulties, passing from one step of success to another, forming new wishes and seeing them gratified.

Samuel Johnson (1709-1784)
English lexicographer, critic and writer

The great pleasure of a dog is that you may make a fool of yourself with him and not only will he not scold you, but he will make a fool of himself too.

Samuel Butler (1835-1902)
English writer

Only one hour in the normal day is more pleasurable than the hour spent in bed with a book before going to sleep, and that is the hour spent in bed with a book after being called in the morning.

Rose Macauley (1881-1958)
English novelist and essayist

Whenever you are sincerely pleased you are nourished.

Ralph Waldo Emerson (1803-1882)
American essayist, poet and philosopher

Pleasure for an hour, a bottle of wine; pleasure for a year, marriage; pleasure for a lifetime, a garden.

Chinese saying

— POSSIBILITY —

The only way to discover the limits of the possible is to go beyond them, to the impossible.

Arthur C. Clarke (1917-)
English science fiction writer

All things are possible until they are proved impossible — and even the impossible may only be so, as of now.

Pearl S. Buck (1892-1973)
American novelist

If I were to wish for anything, I should not wish for wealth and power, but for the passionate sense of the potential, for the eye which, ever young and ardent, sees the possible. Pleasure disappoints, possibility never.

Soren Kierkegaard (1813-1855)
Danish philosopher

— POTENTIAL —

Treat people as if they were what they ought to be and you help them to become what they are capable of being.

Johann Wolfgang von Goethe (1749-1832)
German poet, novelist and playwright

The greater the contrast, the greater the potential. Great energy only comes from a correspondingly great tension between opposites.

Carl Jung (1875-1961)
Swiss psychiatrist

To be what we are, and to become what we are capable of becoming is the only end of life.

Robert Louis Stevenson (1850-1894)
Scottish author and poet

— POVERTY —

The more you have, the more you are occupied,
the less you give. But the less you have, the more
free you are. Poverty for us is a freedom.

Mother Teresa of Calcutta (1910-)
Yugoslav-born missionary

— POWER —

Knowing others is intelligence; knowing yourself
is true wisdom.
Mastering others is strength; mastering yourself
is true power.

Lao-Tzu (c. 604 BC)
Chinese philosopher and founder of Taoism

I cannot do everything, but I can do something.
One person *can* make a difference.

Anonymous

— PRAISE —

I can live for two months on a good compliment.

Mark Twain (1835-1910)
American writer and humorist

Give credit where it's due.

Proverb

Once in a century a man may be ruined or made insufferable by praise. But surely once a minute something generous dies for want of it.

John Masefield (1878-1967)
English poet.

Some natures are too good to be spoiled by praise.

Ralph Waldo Emerson (1803-1882)
American essayist, poet and philosopher

— PRAYER —

More things are wrought by prayer than this
world dreams of.

Alfred, Lord Tennyson (1809-1892)
English poet

Ask, and it shall be given to you; seek and ye shall
find; knock and it shall be opened to you.

Matthew 7:7

Teach me to feel another's woe,
To hide the fault I see,
That mercy I to others show,
That mercy show to me.

Alexander Pope (1788-1744)
English poet

When you prayest, rather let thy heart be
without words than thy words without heart.

John Bunyan (1628-1688)
English writer and moralist

You pray in your distress and in your need,
would that you might also pray in the fullness of
your joy and your days of abundance.

Kahlil Gibran (1883-1931)
Lebanese writer, artist and mystic

Prayer is not an old woman's idle amusement.
Properly understood and applied it is the most
potential instrument of action.

Mahatma Gandhi (1869-1948)
Indian leader., moral teacher and reformer

Oh Lord, help me
To be calm when things go wrong,
To persevere when things are difficult,
To be helpful to those in need,
And to be sympathetic to those whose
hearts are heavy.

Anonymous

— PRESENT JOYS —

Gather ye rosebuds while ye may,
Old time is still a-flying:
And this same flower that smiles today
Tomorrow will be dying.

Robert Herrick (1591-1674)
English poet

Ask not what tomorrow may bring, but count as
blessing every day that Fate allows you.

Horace (65-8 BC)
Roman poet

I try to make the here and now as heavenly as
possible, in case there isn't one to ascend into
when we're done. It's a kind of insurance.

Michael Caine (1933-)
English actor

— PROBLEMS —

First ask yourself, is this my problem? If it isn't, leave it alone. If it is my problem, can I tackle it now? Do so. If your problem could be settled by an expert in some field, go quickly to him and take his advice.

Dr Austen Riggs

I'm grateful for all my problems. As each of them was overcome I became stronger and more able to meet those yet to come. I grew on my difficulties.

J.C. Penney (1875-1971)
American retailing magnate

I could do nothing without problems, they toughen my mind. In fact I tell my assistants not to bring me their successes for they weaken me; but rather to bring me their problems, for they strengthen me.

Charles Franklin Kettering (1876-1958)
American engineer and inventor

— PROCRASTINATION —

I have spent my days stringing and unstringing
my instrument, while the song I came to sing
remains unsung.

Rabindranath Tagore (1861-1941)
Indian poet and philosopher

Procrastination is the thief of time.

Edward Young (1683-1765)
English poet

Wasted days can never be recalled.

Anonymous

Q

– QUIET –

When you become quiet, it just dawns on you.

Thomas A. Edison (1847–1931)
American inventor

In the rush and noise of life, as you have
intervals, step home within yourselves and be
still. Wait upon God, and feel his good presence;
this will carry you evenly through your
day's business.

William Penn (1644–1718)
English Quaker and founder of Pennsylvania, USA

The good and the wise lead quiet lives.

Euipides (480–406 BC)
Greek dramatist

R

— RECEPTIVENESS —

Let us not therefore go hurrying about and
collecting honey, bee-like, buzzing here and
there impatiently from a knowledge of what is to
be arrived at. But let us open out leaves like a
flower, and be passive and receptive: budding
patiently under the eye of Apollo and taking hints
from every noble insect that favours us with
a visit.

John Keats (1795-1821)
English poet

The rain falls on all the fields, but crops grow
only in those that have been tilled and sown.

Chinese saying

— REGRET —

To regret one's own experiences is to arrest one's own development. To deny one's own experiences is to put a lie into the lips of one's own life. It is no less than a denial of the soul.

Oscar Wilde (1854-1900)
Irish poet, wit and dramatist

Make the most of your regrets...To regret deeply is to live afresh.

Henry David Thoreau (1817-1862)
American essayist, poet and mystic

What's gone and what's past help
Should be past grief.

William Shakespeare (1564-1616)
English playwright and poet

— RELATIONSHIP —

Only in relationship can you know yourself, not
in abstraction, and certainly not in isolation.

Jiddu Krishnamurti (1895-1986)
Indian theosophist

Once the realisation is accepted that even
between the closest human beings infinite
distances continue to exist, a wonderful living
side-by-side can grow up, if they succeed in
loving the distance between them, which makes it
possible for each to see the other whole
against a wide sky.

Rainer Maria Rilke (1875-1926)
Austrian poet

The worst sin towards our fellow creatures is not
to hate them, but to be indifferent to them; that's
the essence of inhumanity.

George Bernard Shaw (1856-1950)
Irish dramatist, essayist and critic

I do my thing, and you do your thing,
I am not in this world to live up to
your expectations
And you are not in this world to live up to mine.
You are you and I am I,
And if by chance we find each other,
it's beautiful.
If not, it can't be helped.

Frederick (Fritz) Salomon Perls (1893-1970)
German-born American psychologist

Personal relations are the important thing for
ever and ever, and not this outer life of telegrams
and anger.

E.M. Forster (1879-1970)
English novelist

I am a part of all that I have met.

Alfred, Lord Tennyson (1809-1892)
English poet

— RELIGION —

There is only one religion, though there are a hundred versions of it.

George Bernard Shaw (1856-1950)
Irish dramatist, essayist and critic

Be a good human being, a warm-hearted affectionate person. That is my fundamental belief. Having a sense of caring, a feeling of compassion will bring happiness or peace of mind to oneself and automatically create a positive atmosphere.

Dalai Lama (1935-)
Tibetan spiritual leader

Show love to all creatures and thou will be happy; for when thou lovest all things, thou lovest the Lord, for he is all in all.

Tulsi Das Hindu spiritual tradition

He who is filled with love is filled with
God himself.

St Augustine of Hippo (347-430 AD)

I consider myself a Hindu, Christian, Moslem,
Jew, Budhist and Confucian.

Mahatma Gandhi (1869-1948)
Indian leader, moral teacher and reformer

The worst moment for the atheist is when he is
really thankful, and has nobody to thank.

Dante Gabriel Rossetti (1828-1882)
English poet and painter

One man finds religion in his literature and
science; another finds it in his joy and his duty.

Joseph Joubert (1754-1824)
French writer

— REPUTATION —

The only time you realise you have a reputation
is when you fail to live up to it.

Anonymous

— RESILIENCE —

If you fell down yesterday, stand up today.

H.G. Wells (1866~1946)
English author

— REVOLUTION —

Revolution is the festival of the oppressed.

Germaine Greer (1939~)
Australian writer and feminist

— RIGHTEOUSNESS —

If there be righteousness in the heart, there will
be beauty in the character.
If there be beauty in the character, there will be
harmony in the home.
If there be harmony in the home, there will be
order in the nation.
If there be order in the nation, there will be
peace in the world.

Confucius (551-479 BC)
Chinese philosopher

I must stand with anybody that stands right,
stand with him while he is right, and part with
him when he goes wrong.

Abraham Lincoln (1809-1865)
President of the United States, 1861-1865

Right is might.

Anonymous

264

— RISK —

And the trouble is, if you don't risk anything, you risk even more.

Erica Jong (1942-)
American novelist and poet

Don't refuse to go on an occasional wild goose chase. That's what wild geese are for.

Anonymous

Risk! Risk anything! Care no more for the opinions of others, for those voices. Do the hardest thing on earth for you. Act for yourself. Face the truth.

Katherine Mansfield (1888-1923)
New Zealand author

Risk is what separates the good part of life from the tedium.

Jimmy Zero
American musician

S

— SAFETY —

The desire for safety stands against every great
and noble enterprise.

Publius Cornelius Tacitus (55-120 AD)
Roman historian

It is always safe to learn, even from our enemies;
seldom safe to venture to instruct, even
our friends.

Charles Caleb Colton (1780-1832)
English clergyman and author

The only way to be absolutely safe is never to try
anything for the first time.

Magnus Pyke (1908-)
English scientist

— *SELF-CONFIDENCE* —

Self-confidence is the first requisite to great undertakings.

Samuel Johnson (1709-1784)
English lexicographer, critic and writer

Self-trust is the first secret of success.

Ralph Waldo Emerson (1803-1882)
American poet and essayist

Those who believe they are exclusively in the right are generally those who achieve something.

Aldous Huxley (1894-1963)
English novelist and essayist

You can get good fish and chips at the Savoy; and you can put up with fancy people once you understand that you don't have to be like them.

Gracie Fields (1888-1979)
English singer

— SELF-CONTROL —

Just as a bicycle chain may be too tight, so may one's carefulness and conscientiousness be so tense as to hinder the running of one's mind.

William James (1842-1910)
American psychologist and philosopher

If your aim is control, it must be self-control first. If your aim is management, it must be self-management first.

Anonymous

Self-command is the main elegance.

Ralph Waldo Emerson (1803-1882)
American essayist, poet and philosopher

— *SELF-DISCOVERY* —

Learn to get in touch with the silence within
yourself and know that everything in this life has
a purpose.

Elisabeth Kubler-Ross (1926 ~)
Swiss-born American psychiatrist

Just trust yourself, then you will know how
to live.

Johann Wolfgang von Goethe (1749~1832)
German poet, novelist and playwright

Once read thy own breast right,
And thou hast done with fears!
Man gets no other light,
Search he a thousand years.

Matthew Arnold (1822~1888)
English poet and critic

Pearls lie not on the seashore. If thou desirest one thou must dive for it.

Chinese proverb

In meditation it is possible to dive deeper into the mind to a place where there is no disturbance and there is absolute solitude. It is at this point in the profound stillness that the sound of the mind can be heard.

A.E.I. Falconar (1926-)
Indian-born philosopher

There is only one journey. Going inside yourself.

Rainer Maria Rilke (1875-1926)
Austrian poet

No one remains quite what he was, once he recognizes himself.

Thomas Mann (1875-1955)
German novelist

— SELFLESSNESS —

To give and not to count the cost;
To fight and not to heed the wounds;
To toil and not to seek for rest;
To labour and not ask for any reward
Save that of knowing that we do Thy will.

St Ignatius Loyola (1491-1556)
Spanish priest

Where self exists, God is not;
Where God exists there is no self.

Sikh morning prayer

Inwardness, mildness and self-renouncement do
make for man's happiness.

Matthew Arnold (1822-1888)
English poet and critic

— SELF-RESPECT —

Let us not forget that a man can never get away from himself.

Johann Wolfgang von Goethe (1749-1832)
German poet, novelist and playwright

No-one can make you feel inferior without your consent.

Eleanor Roosevelt (1884-1962)
First Lady of the United States, 1933-1945

It is difficult to make a man miserable while he feels he is worthy of himself.

Abraham Lincoln (1809-1865)
President of the United States of America, 1861-1865

If you put a small value upon yourself, rest assured that the world will not raise it.

Anonymous

A man cannot be comfortable without his
own approval.

Mark Twain (1835-1910)
American writer and humorist

I think somehow we learn who we really are and
then live with that decision.

Eleanor Roosevelt (1884-1961)
First Lady of the United States, 1933-1945

Self-respecting people do not care to peep at
their reflections in unexpected mirrors, or to see
themselves as others see them.

Logan Pearsall Smith (1865-1946)
English writer

— SILENCE —

Well-timed silence hath more eloquence
than speech.

Martin Farquhar Tupper (1810-1889)
English writer

★

— SINCERITY —

What comes from the heart, goes to the heart.

Samuel Taylor Coleridge (1772-1834)
English poet

What's a man's first duty? The answer's brief: to
be himself.

Henrik Ibsen (1828-1906)
Norwegian dramatist

— SMILE —

It takes seventy-two muscles to frown, but only thirteen to smile.

Anonymous

Smile at each other; smile at your wife, smile at your husband, smile at your children, smile at each other — it doesn't matter who it is — and that will help you to grow up in greater love for each other.

Mother Teresa of Calcutta (1910-)
Yugoslav-born missionary

A smile breaks down most barriers.

Anonymous

— *SOLITUDE* —

He who does not enjoy solitude will not love freedom.

Artur Schopenhauer (1788-1860)
German philosopher

I had three chairs in my house; one for solitude, two for friendship, three for society.

Henry David Thoreau (1817-1862)
American essayist, poet and mystic

Solitude is as needful to the imagination as society is wholesome for the character.

James Russell Lowell (1819-1891)
American poet, essayist and diplomat

Solitary trees, if they grow at all, grow strong.

Sir Winston Churchill (1874-1965)
English statesman

O Solitude, the soul's best friend,
That man acquainted with himself dost make.

Charles Cotton (1630-1687)
English poet

✸

Go cherish your soul; expel companions; set your
habits to a life of solitude; then will the faculties
rise fair and full within.

Ralph Waldo Emerson (1803-1882)
American essayist, poet and philosopher

✸

Living in solitude till the fullness of time, I still
kept the dew of my youth and the freshness of
my heart.

Nathaniel Hawthorne (1804-1864)
American novelist and short story writer

✸

I never found the companion that was so
companionable as solitude.

Henry David Thoreau (1817-1862)
American essayist, poet and mystic

I am sure of this, that by going much alone, a man will get more of a noble courage in thought and word than from all the wisdom that is in books.

Ralph Waldo Emerson (1803-1882)
American essayist, poet and philosopher

Solitude is the nurse of enthusiasm, and enthusiasm is the true parent of genius.

Isaac D'Israeli (1766-1848)
English literary critic

– *SOLUTION* –

Every problem contains the seeds of its own solution.

Anonymous

— SORROW —

Truly, it is in the darkness that one finds the light,
so when we are in sorrow, then this light is
nearest of all to us.

Johannes Eckhart (c.1260-1327)
German mystic

One often calms one's grief by recounting it.

Pierre Corneille (1606-1684)
French dramatist

Pure and complete sorrow is as impossible as
pure and complete joy.

Leo Tolstoy (1828-1910)
Russian novelist

Blessed are they that mourn, for they shall
be comforted.

Matthew 5:4

— STRENGTH —

You must be the anvil or the hammer.

Johann Wolfgang von Goethe (1749-1832)
German poet, novelist and playwright

Be strong and courageous, and do the work.

Chronicles 28:20

The world breaks everyone and afterwards many
are strong at the broken places.

Ernest Hemingway (1899-1961)
American novelist

You who perceive yourself as weak and frail,
with futile hopes and devastated dreams, born
but to die, to weep and suffer pain, hear this: all
power is given unto you in earth and heaven.
There is nothing you cannot do.

A Course in Miracles

— STRUGGLE —

It seems to me that one of the greatest stumbling blocks in life is this constant struggle to reach, to achieve, to acquire.

Jiddu Krishnamurti (1895-1986)
Indian theosophist

Better that we should die fighting than be outraged and dishonoured...Better to die than live in slavery.

Emmeline Pankhurst (1858-1928)
Suffragette leader

The struggle that is not joyous is the wrong struggle. The joy of the struggle is not hedonism and hilarity, but the sense of purpose, achievement and dignity which is the reflowering of etiolated energy.

Germaine Greer (1939-)
Australian writer and feminist

Resistance to tyrants is obedience to God.

Benjamin Franklin (1706-1790)
American statesman and philosopher

Our greatest glory is not in never falling, but in rising every time we fall.

Confucius (551-479 BC)
Chinese philosopher

If a man lives without inner struggle, if everything happens in him without opposition...he will remain such as he is.

G.I. Gurdjieff (1877-1949)
Russian mystic and teacher of the occult

Golf without bunkers and hazards would be lame. So would life.

B.C. Forbes (1880-1954)
American writer

— *SUCCESS* —

Singleness of purpose is one of the chief essentials for success in life, no matter what may be one's aim.

John D. Rockefeller, Jr. (1874-1960)
American oil millionaire and philanthropist

I never allow any difficulties. The great secret of being useful and successful is to admit no difficulties.

Sir George Gipps (1791-1847)
Governor of New South Wales, 1838-1846

If one advances confidently in the direction of his dreams, and endeavours to live the life which he had imagined, he will meet with a success unexpected in common hours.

Henry David Thoreau (1817-1862)
American essayist, poet and mystic

Success consists of getting up just one more time than you fall.

Anonymous

The only place where success comes before work is a dictionary.

Vidal Sassoon (1928-)
English hair stylist

A lot of successful people are risk-takers. Unless you're willing to do that...to have a go, fail miserably, and have another go, success won't happen.

Phillip Adams (1939-)
Australian author, writer and radio broadcaster

The secret of success is making your vocation your vacation.

Mark Twain (1835-1910)
American writer and humorist

There is only one success — to be able to spend your life in your own way.

Christopher Darlington Morley (1890-1957)
American novelist and essayist

If you want to succeed you should strike out on new paths, rather than travel the worn paths of accepted success.

John D. Rockefeller (1839-1937)
American oil millionaire monopolist and philanthropist

Success is to be measured not so much by the position one has reached in life, as by the obstacles which one has overcome while trying to succeed.

Booker Taliaferro Washington (1856-1915)
American teacher, writer and speaker

There are no gains without pains.

Adlai Stevenson (1900-1965)
American statesman

Do what you love and believe in, and success will
come naturally.

Anonymous

I cannot give you the formula for success, but I
can give you the formula for failure —
which is: try to please everybody.

Herbert Bayard Swope (1882-1958)
American newspaper editor

The toughest thing about success is that you've
got to keep on being a success.

Irving Berlin (1888-1989)
American composer

What's money? A man is a success if he gets up in the morning and goes to bed at night and in between does what he wants to do.

Bob Dylan (1941-)
American singer and songwriter

I've never sought success in order to get fame and money; it's the talent and the passion that count in success.

Ingrid Bergman (1915-1982)
Swedish-born actress

Getting ahead in a difficult profession requires avid faith in yourself. You must be able to sustain yourself against staggering blows and unfair reversals.

Sophia Loren (1934-)
Italian actress

The door to success has two signs,
Push — and Pull.

Leo Rosten's Treasury of Jewish Quotations

It is no good saying 'we are doing our best.' You have got to succeed in doing what is necessary.

Winston Churchill (1874-1965)
English statesman

What is success?
To laugh often and much;
To win the respect of intelligent people and the affection of children;
To earn the appreciation of honest critics and endure the betrayal of false friends;
To appreciate beauty;
To find the best in others;
To leave the world a bit better, whether by a healthy child, a garden patch or a redeemed social condition;
To know even one life has breathed easier because you have lived;
This is to have succeeded.

Ralph Waldo Emerson (1803-1882)
American essayist, poet and philosopher

— *SUFFERING* —

My personal trials have taught me the value of
unmerited suffering. As my sufferings mounted I
soon realised that there were two ways that I
could respond to my situation: either to react
with bitterness or seek to transform the suffering
into a creative force.

Martin Luther King (1929-1968)
American black civil-rights leader

— *SUPERIORITY* —

There is nothing noble about being superior to
some other man. The true nobility lies in being
superior to your previous self.

Hindu proverb

T

— TALENT —

Everyone has talent. What is rare is the courage
to follow the talent to the dark place where
it leads.

Erica Jong (1942-)
American novelist and poet

All our talents increase in the using, and every
faculty, both good and bad, strengthen
by exercise.

Anne Brontë (1820-1849)
English writer and poet

Conciseness is the sister of talent.

Anton Chekhov (1860-1904)
Russian writer

— TALK —

Who is there that can make muddy water clear?
But if allowed to remain still, it will gradually
become clear of itself...Be sparing of speech, and
things will come right of themselves.

Lao-Tzu (c. 604 BC)
Chinese philosopher and founder of Taoism

I don't care how much a man talks, if he only
says it in a few words.

Josh Billings (1818-1885)
American humorist

Talking and eloquence are not the same: to
speak, and to speak well, are two things.

Ben Jonson (1573-1637)
English dramatist

When you have nothing to say, say nothing.

Charles Caleb Colton (1780-1832)
English clergyman, sportsman, gambler and author

To talk is our chief business in this world, and talk is by far the most accessible pleasure. It costs nothing in money; it is all profit, it completes education, founds and fosters friendships, and can be enjoyed at any age and in almost any state of health.

Robert Louis Stevenson (1850-1894)
Scottish novelist, poet and essayist

The fact that people are born with two eyes and two ears but only one tongue suggests that they ought to look and listen twice as much as they speak.

Anonymous

— TEACHING —

It is the supreme art of the teacher to awaken joy
in creative expression and knowledge.

Albert Einstein (1879-1955)
German-born physicist

— TEARS —

The soul would have no rainbow
Had the eyes no tears.

John Vance Cheney (1848-1922)
American poet

The liquid drops of tears that you have shed
Shall come again, transform'd to orient pearl,
Advantaging their loan with interest
Of ten times double gain of happiness.

William Shakespeare (1564-1616)
English playwright and poet

★

— THANKS —

When you arise in the morning
Give thanks for the morning light.
Give thanks for your life and strength.
Give thanks for your food
And give thanks for the joy of living.
And if perchance you see no reason for
giving thanks,
Rest assured the fault is in yourself.

American Indian saying

Myself in constant good health, and in a
handsome and thriving condition. Blessed be
Almighty God for it.

Samuel Pepys (1633-1703)
English diarist

— THOUGHTS —

You may believe that you are responsible for
what you do, but not for what you think. The
truth is that you are responsible for what you
think, because it is only at this level that you can
exercise choice. What you do comes from what
you think.

A Course in Miracles

A man is what he thinks about all day long.

Ralph Waldo Emerson (1803-1882)
American essayist, poet and philosopher

Every thought you have makes up some segment
of the world you see. It is with your thoughts,
then, that we must work, if your perception of
the world is to be changed.

A Course in Miracles

The most immutable barrier in nature is between
one man's thoughts and another's.

William James (1842-1910)
American psychologist and philosopher

Thinking is the hardest work there is, which is
probably why so few engage in it.

Henry Ford (1863-1947)
American motor car manufacturer

Mind is everything; we become what we think.

Buddha (5th century BC)
Founder of Buddhism

The mind is never right but when it is at peace
within itself.

Seneca (4 BC-65 AD)
Roman philosopher and statesman

A great many people think they are thinking
when they are merely rearranging
their prejudices.

William James (1842-1910)
American psychologist and philosopher

Every revolution was first a thought in one
man's mind.

Ralph Waldo Emerson (1803-1882)
American essayist, poet and philosopher

Life does not consist mainly — or even largely —
of facts and happenings. It consists mainly of the
storm of thoughts that are forever blowing
through one's mind.

Mark Twain (1835-1910)
American writer and humorist

— TIME —

Don't serve time, make time serve you.

Willie Sutton (1860~1928)
American educationist

Dost thou love life? Then do not squander time;
for that's the stuff life is made of.

Benjamin Franklin (1706~1790)
American statesman and philosopher

Your time may be limited, but your imagination
is not.

Anonymous

These trying times are the good old days we'll be
longing for in a few years.

José Ferrer (1909~1992)
American actor

There is a time to be born, and a time to die, says
Solomon, and it is a memento of a truly wise
man; but there is an interval of infinte
importance between these two times.

Leigh Richmond (1772-1827)
English writer

Take time to think...it is the source of power.
Take time to play...it is the secret of
perpetual youth.
Take time to read...it is the fountain of wisdom.
Take time to pray...it is the greatest power
on earth.
Take time to laugh...it is the music of the soul.
Take time to give...it is too short a day to
be selfish.

Anonymous

It is familiarity with life that makes time speed quickly. When every day is a step into the unknown, as for children, the days are long with the gathering of experience.

George Robert Gissing (1857-1903)
English novelist

Lose an hour in the morning and you will be all day hunting for it.

Richard Whately (1787-1863)
English Archbishop of Dublin

You have to live on this twenty-four hours of daily time. Out of it you have to spin health, pleasure, money, content, respect and the evolution of your immortal soul. Its right use, its most effective use, is a matter of the highest urgency and of the most thrilling actuality. All depends on that. We shall never have any more time.

Arnold Bennett (1867-1931)
English novelist

Time goes, you say? Ah no! Alas,
Time stays, *we* go.

Henry Austin Dobson (1840-1921)
English poet

Let us spend one day as deliberately as nature,
and not be thrown off the track by every nutshell
and mosquito's wing that falls on the rails. Let us
rise early and fast, or break fast, gently and
without perturbation; let company come and let
company go, let the bells ring and the children
cry — determined to make a day of it. If the
engine whistles, let it whistle till it is hoarse for
its pains. If the bell rings, why should we run?
Time is but the stream I go a-fishing in.

Henry David Thoreau (1817-1862)
American essayist and poet

Time is what we want most, but what, alas, we
use worst.

William Penn (1644-1718)
English Quaker and founder of Pennsylvania, USA

An inch of gold will not buy an inch of time.

Chinese proverb

If only I could stand on a street corner with my hat in my hand, and get people to throw their wasted time into it!

Bernard Berenson (1865-1959)
American art critic

The future is something which everyone reaches at the rate of sixty minutes an hour, whatever he does, whoever he is.

C.S. Lewis (1898-1963)
Irish-born academic, writer and poet

We have to make the most of every secondo.

David Helfgott (1947-)
Australian concert pianist

Time is
Too slow for those who wait,
Too swift for those who fear,
Too long for those who grieve,
Too short for those who rejoice,
But for those who love, time is
Eternity. Hours fly, flowers die,
New days, new ways, pass by.
Love stays.

Sundial inscription

The busier you are, the more you find time to do
— and vice versa.

Anonymous

Our todays and yesterdays are the blocks with
which we build.

Henry Wadsworth Longfellow (1807-1882)
American poet

— TODAY & TOMORROW —

Look to this day...In it lies all the realities and
verities of existence, the bliss of growth, the
splendour of action, the glory of power. For
yesterday is but a dream and tomorrow is only a
vision. But today, well-lived, makes every
yesterday a dream of happiness and every
tomorrow a vision of hope.

Sanskrit proverb

Happy the man, and happy he alone,
He who can call today his own:
He who, secure within, can say
Tomorrow do thy worst, for I have lived today.

John Dryden (1631–1700)
English poet

Don't start living tomorrow — tomorrow never
arrives. Start working on your dreams and
ambitions today.

Anonymous

The bud of a rose is just as beautiful as the full
bloom. Appreciate what you have at
the moment.

Anonymous

Carpe diem. (Seize the day.)

Horace (65-8 BC)
Roman poet

It's only when we truly know and understand
that we have a limited time on earth — and that
we have no way of knowing when our time is up
— that we will begin to live each day to the
fullest, as if it was the only one we had.

Elisabeth Kubler-Ross (1926-)
Swiss-born American psychiatrist

What's lost today may be won tomorrow.

Miguel de Cervantes (1547-1616)
Spanish writer

After all, tomorrow is another day.

Margaret Mitchell (1900-1949)
American novelist

There is left for myself but one day in the week
— today. Any man can fight the battles of
today...It isn't the experiences of today that drives
men mad. It is the remorse for something that
happened yesterday, and the dread of what
tomorrow may disclose.

Robert J. Burdette (1844-1914)
American humorist

One today is worth two tomorrows; never leave
that till tomorrow which you can do today.

Benjamin Franklin (1706-1790)
American statesman and philosopher

— TOLERANCE —

Tolerance not only saves others from your prejudices and fears, but frees your soul to explore and accept the world that has been given to you.

Anonymous

Give to every other human being every right that you claim for yourself.

Robert G. Ingersoll (1833-1899)
American lawyer and orator

— TRANSFORMATION —

The meeting of two personalities is like the contact of two chemical substances: if there is any reaction, both are transformed.

Carl Jung (1875-1961)
Swiss psychiatrist

— TRAVEL —

Travel is fatal to prejudice, bigotry, and
narrow-mindedness.

Mark Twain (1835-1910)
American writer and humorist

Travel and change of place impart new vigour
to the mind.

Seneca (4 BC-65 AD)
Roman philosopher

Everyone's travels through life end the same way,
so you might as well enjoy the journey.

Anonymous

The soul of a journey is liberty, perfect liberty, to
think, feel, do just as one pleases.

William Hazlitt (1778-1830)
English essayist

— TRUTH —

The truth hurts like a thorn at first; but in the
end it blossoms like a rose.

Samuel Ha-Nagid (c. 900)
Jewish scholar

Men stumble over the truth from time to time,
but most pick themselves up and hurry off as if
nothing happened.

Sir Winston Churchill (1874-1965)
English statesman

It takes two to speak the truth — one to speak,
and another to hear.

Henry David Thoreau (1817-1862)
American essayist, poet and mystic

Nothing gives us rest but the sincere search for
truth.

Blaise Pascal (1623-1662)
French physicist, theologian and writer

Rather than love, than money, than fame,
give me truth.

Henry David Thoreau (1817-1862)
American essayist, poet and mystic

If you do not tell the truth about yourself you
cannot tell it about other people.

Virginia Woolf (1882-1941)
English writer

Truth is within ourselves; it takes no rise
From outward things, whate'er you may believe.
There is an inmost centre in us all,
Where truth abides in fullness.

Robert Browning (1812-1889)
English poet

The man who speaks the truth is always at ease.

Persian proverb

The truth is cruel, but it can be loved and it
makes free those who love it.

George Santayana (1863-1952)
Spanish philosopher, poet and novelist

It is good to know the truth and speak it, but it is
better to talk of palm trees.

Chinese proverb

— TRYING —

Until you try, you don't know what you can't do.

Henry James (1843-1916)
American novelist

U

— UNDERSTANDING —

A single moment of understanding can flood a whole life with meaning.

Anonymous

If one is master of one thing and understands one thing well, one has at the same time insight into and understanding of many things.

Vincent Van Gogh (1853~1890)
Dutch post~impressionist painter

— UNIQUE —

All cases are unique, and very similar to others.

T.S. Eliot (1888~1965)
American-born poet and dramatist

V

— VICTORY —

He...got the better of himself, and that's the best
kind of victory one can wish for.

Miguel de Cervantes (1547-1616)
Spanish author

— VIRTUE —

Virtue is never left to stand alone. He who has it
will have neighbours.

Confucius (551-479 BC)
Chinese philosopher

W

– WEALTH –

Lazy men are soon poor.

Proverb

Wealth is a good servant, but a bad master.

Anonymous

Be not penny-wise; riches have wings and
sometimes they fly away of themselves;
sometimes they must be sent flying to bring
in more.

Francis Bacon (1561–1626)
English philosopher

— WINNING —

An integral part of being a star is having the will
to win. All the champions have it.

Betty Cuthbert (1938-)
Australian Olympic gold-medal sprinter

Only a loser finds it impossible to accept a
temporary set-back. A winner asks why.

Ita Buttrose (1942-)
Media personality

You have to make more noise than anyone else,
you have to make yourself more obtrusive than
anyone else, you have to fill all the papers more
than anyone else, in fact you have to be there all
the time...if you are really going to get your
reform realised.

Emmeline Pankhurst (1858-1928)
Suffragette leader

— WISDOM —

Be wiser than other people if you can, but do not
tell them so.

Earl of Chesterfield (1694-1773)
English statesman

True wisdom consists in knowing one's duty
exactly. True piety in acting what one knows. To
aim at more than this, is to run into
endless mistakes.

Bishop Thomas Wilson (1663-1755)
English churchman

In seeking wisdom, the first step is silence, the
second listening, the third remembering, the
fourth practising, the fifth — teaching others.

Ibn Gabirol (Avicebron) (1020-c.1070)
Jewish poet and philosopher

Knowledge comes, but wisdom lingers.

Alfred, Lord Tennyson (1809-1892)
English poet

I don't think much of a man who is not wiser
today than he was yesterday.

Abraham Lincoln (1809-1865)
President of the United States, 1861-1865

A wise man hears one word and
understands two.

Jewish proverb

The foolish man wonders at the unusual, but the
wise man at the usual.

Ralph Waldo Emerson (1803-1882)
American essayist, poet and philosopher

Be with wise men and become wise.

Proverbs 13:20

The wisdom of the wise, and the experience of
the ages, may be preserved by quotations.

Isaac D'Israeli (1766-1848)
English literary critic

He who knows others is learned; he who knows
himself is wise.

Lao-Tze (c. 604 BC)
Chinese philosopher and founder of Taoism

It is the province of knowledge to speak and it is
the privilege of wisdom to listen.

Oliver Wendell Holmes (1809-1894)
American writer

Every man is a damn fool for at least five minutes every day; wisdom consists in not exceeding the limit.

Elbert Hubbard (1856-1915)
American writer

The price of wisdom is above rubies.

Job 28:18

Nine-tenths of wisdom is being wise in time

Theodore Roosevelt (1858-1919)
President of the United States, 1901-1912

It is characteristic of wisdom not to do desperate things.

Henry David Thoreau (1817-1862)
American essayist, poet and mystic

— WORDS —

Try to say the very thing you really mean, the
whole of it, nothing more or less or other than
what you really mean. That is the whole art and
joy of words.

C.S. Lewis (1898~1963)
Irish-born academic, writer and poet.

Man does not live by words alone, despite the
fact that sometimes he has to eat them.

Broderick Crawford (1911-)
American actor

— WORK —

To my mind the best investment a young man
starting out in business could possibly make is to
give all his time, all his energies to work, just
plain, hard work.

Charles M. Schwab (1862-1939)
American industrialist

The glory of a workman, still more of a
master-workman, that he does his work well,
ought to be his most precious possession; like the
'honour of a soldier', dearer to him than life.

Thomas Carlyle (1795-1881)
Scottish essayist, historian and philosopher

It is impossible to enjoy idling thoroughly unless
one has plenty of work to do.

Jerome K. Jerome (1859-1927)
English playwright and humorist

Choose a job you love, and you will never have to work a day in your life.

Anonymous

What's really important in life? Sitting on the beach? Looking at television eight hours a day? I think we have to appreciate that we're alive for only a limited period of time, and we'll spend most of our lives working. That being the case, I believe one of the most important priorities is to do whatever we do as well as we can. We should take pride in that.

Victor Kermit Kiam (1926-)
American corporate executive

The force, the mass of character, mind, heart or soul that a man can put into any work, is the most important factor in that work.

A.P. Peabody (1811-1893)
American writer

The highest reward for man's toil is not what he gets for it but what he becomes by it.

John Ruskin (1819-1900)
English writer and art critic

Whatsoever thy hand findeth to do, do it with thy might.

Ecclesiastes

Work is love made visible.

Kahlil Gibran (1883-1931)
Lebanese poet, author, artist and mystic

Nothing is really work unless you would rather be doing something else.

J.M. Barrie (1860-1937)
Scottish novelist

In order that people may be happy in their work, these three things are needed: They must be fit for it. They must not do too much of it. And they must have a sense of success in it.

John Ruskin (1819-1900)
English writer and art critic

Well begun is half done.

Proverb

The more one works, the more willing one is to work.

Lord Chesterfield (1694-1773)
English statesman and author

It is work that gives flavour to life.

Henri-Frederic Amiel (1828-1881)
Swiss philosopher and critic

There is no substitute for hard work.

Thomas A. Edison (1847~1931)
American inventor

To generous souls, every task is noble.

Euripides (480~406 BC)
Greek dramatist

No race can prosper till it learns that there is as
much dignity in tilling a field as in writing
a poem.

Booker Taliaferro Washington (1856~1915)
American teacher; writer and speaker

— WORRY —

I've found that worry and irritation vanish into thin air the moment I open my mind to the many blessings I possess.

Dale Carnegie (1888~1955)
American author and lecturer

As a cure for worrying, work is better than whisky.

Thomas A. Edison (1845~1931)
American inventor

I have spent most of my life worrying about things that have never happened.

Mark Twain (1835~1910)
American writer and humorist

I am an old man and have had many troubles, but most of them never happened.

Anonymous

You're only here for a short visit. Don't hurry.
Don't worry. And be sure to smell the flowers
along the way.

Walter C. Hagen (1892-1969)
American golfer

Worry is interest paid on trouble before it
falls due.

William Inge (1860-1954)
English prelate and author

Worries go down better with soup than without.

Jewish proverb

Y

— YES —

Where we are free to act, we are free to refrain
from acting, and where we are able to say no, we
are also able to say yes.

Aristotle (384-322 BC)
Greek philosopher

Say yes to life.

Anonymous

For what has been — thanks!
For what shall be — yes!

Dag Hammarskjold (1905-1961)
Swedish diplomat

– YOU –

Always be a first-rate version of yourself, instead
of a second-rate version of somebody else.

Judy Garland (1922-1969)
American singer

You have to live with yourself, so it's important
that you are fit for yourself to know.

Anonymous

Don't compromise yourself. You are all
you've got.

Janis Joplin (1943-1970)
American singer and songwriter

If I try to be like him, who will be like me?

Jewish proverb

One person's definition of success is another's first step. Only you can rate your accomplishments, and find peace within yourself.

Anonymous

To be nobody but yourself — in a world which is doing its best, night and day, to make you everybody else — means to fight the hardest battle which any human being can fight, and never stop fighting.

e.e. cummings (1894-1962)
English poet

— YOUTH —

Youth is a disease that must be borne with patiently! Time, indeed, will cure it.

R.H. Benson (1871-1914)
English novelist

Z

— ZEAL —

Zeal without knowledge is fire without light.

Thomas Fuller (1608~1661)
English divine and historian

— Subject Index —

More
POCKET
POSITIVES

Compiled by Maggie Pinkney

Contents

Introduction

Mankind would lose half its wisdom built up over centuries if it lost its great sayings. They contain the best parts of the best books.

Thomas Jefferson (1743-1826)

The resounding success of *Pocket Positives* has inspired us to assemble this new anthology of benign and healing thoughts to provide you with encouragement and inspiration. Again, these quotations are drawn from a wide range of sources — including the world's greatest philosophers, religious leaders, poets, novelists and humorists, as well as people from many other walks of life.

What all these men and women — from the distant past to the present — have in common is the ability to inspire us in some way, whether it is with their love, enthusiasm, compassion, courage, wisdom, success or pure zest for life. It's not that they are superhuman. Many quotations reveal that their authors are deeply acquainted with sorrows, failures and fears. But they have managed to keep sight of the larger picture, and to fight back. In fact, one of the most comforting aspects of this anthology is that it shows us that whatever our problems are, we are not alone. Someone else, somewhere, has felt as we do, and has experienced what we are going through. This is in itself a consolation, and certainly helps one to gain an all-important sense of perspective.

In this selection, many themes occur again and again — each time expressed in a fresh new way. For example, Austrian psychiatrist Alfred Adler wrote, 'We can be cured of depression in only fourteen days if every day we will try to think of how we can be helpful to others.' Mark Twain reached the same conclusion: 'The best way to cheer yourself up is to cheer someone else up,' he advised. A similar sentiment is expressed yet again — and with great elegance — by Ralph Waldo Emerson: 'It is one of the most beautiful compensations of this life that no man can sincerely try to help another without helping himself.'

Some of the famous men and women who share their thoughts with us in these 'pocket positives' give us a sense of understanding and acceptance. Others, such as Martin Luther King, Winston Churchill, Aung San Suu Kyi and Helen Keller, inspire us by their example as much as by their words.

Quotations are arranged under subject heads for easy reference, and an index of sources is also included. Keep this companionable anthology by your bedside and read it regularly. It will help you to enjoy a more fulfilling and meaningful life. Simply open it at any page until you find a quote that 'speaks' to you in your present frame of mind. As Albert Einstein said, 'There are two ways to live your life. One is as though nothing is a miracle. The other is as though everything is a miracle.'

Welcome to *More Pocket Positives*!

A

Ability

One of the greatest of all principles is that men can do what they think they can do.

Norman Vincent Peale, 1898-1993
American writer and minister

It is better to have a little ability and use it well than to have much ability and make poor use of it.

Anonymous

They are able who think they are able.

Virgil, 70-19 BC
Roman poet

Achievement

It was a golden year beyond my dreams. I proved you're never too old to achieve what you really want to do.

Heather Turland, b. 1960
Australian women's marathon gold medallist,
Commonwealth Games, 1998

Achievement is largely the product of steadily raising one's level of aspiration and expectation.

Jack Nicklaus, b. 1940
American golfer

All the things we achieve are things we have first of all imagined and then made happen.

David Malouf, b. 1934
Australian writer

Action

To will is to select a goal, determine a course of action that will bring one to that goal, and then hold to that action till the goal is reached. The key is action.

Michael Hanson, 1863-1908
American mathematician

Action is the antidote to despair.

Joan Baez, b. 1941
American folk singer

Well done is better than well said.

Benjamin Franklin, 1706-1790
American statesman and scientist

A little knowledge that *acts* is worth infinitely more than knowledge that is idle.

Kahlil Gibran, 1882-1931
Lebanese poet, artist and mystic

In our era the road to holiness necessarily passes through the world of action.

Dag Hammarskjold, 1905-1961
Swedish statesman and humanitarian

Just go out there and do what you've got to do.

Martina Navratilova, b. 1956
Czechoslovakian-born American tennis champion

Don't wait for a light to appear at the end of the tunnel, stride down there . . . and light the bloody thing yourself.

Sara Henderson, b. 1936
Australian outback station manager and writer

As life is action and passion, it is required of man that he should share the passion and action of his time, at peril of being judged not to have lived.

Oliver Wendell Holmes, 1809-1894
American writer and physician

All mankind is divided into three classes: those that are immovable, those that are movable, and those that move.

Benjamin Franklin, 1706-1790
American statesman and scientist

The shortest answer is doing.

English proverb

A good deed, no matter how small, is worth more than all the good intentions in the world.

Anonymous

You can't build a reputation on what you're going to do.

Henry Ford, 1863-1946
American car manufacturer

Knowledge without Action is useless. Action without Knowledge is foolishness.

Sai Baba
Indian spiritual master

However brilliant an action may be it should not be esteemed great unless the result of a great motive.

Duc de La Rochefoucauld 1613-1680
French writer

Action may not always bring happiness, but there is no happiness without action.

Benjamin Disraeli, 1804-1881
British Prime Minister and writer

How may a man gain self-knowledge? By contemplation? Certainly not; but by action. Try to do your duty and you will find what you are fit for. But what is your duty? The demand of the hour.

Johann von Goethe, 1749-1832
German writer, dramatist and scientist

Our grand business in life is not to see what lies dimly at a distance, but to do what clearly lies at hand.

Thomas Carlyle, 1795-1881
Scottish historian, essayist and critic

Sometimes the only way for me to find out what it is I want to do is go ahead and do something. Then the moment I start to act, my feelings become clear.

Hugh Prather, b. 1938
American writer

The man who does things makes many mistakes, but he never makes the biggest mistake of all — doing nothing.

Benjamin Franklin, 1706-1790
American statesman and scientist

Adventurousness

Not all those that wander are lost.

J. R. R. Tolkien, 1892-1973
English author

Adversity

A man of character finds a special
attractiveness in difficulty, since it is only by
coming to grips with difficulty that he can
realise his potentialities.

Charles de Gaulle, 1890-1970
French statesman and general

A woman is like a teabag — you can't tell how
strong she is until you put her in hot water.

Nancy Reagan, b. 1923
First Lady of the United States of America

Adversity introduces a man to himself.

Anonymous

When you're up to your ears in trouble, try
using the part that isn't submerged.

Anonymous

Advice

If I were asked to give what I consider the single most useful piece of advice for all humanity it would be this: Expect trouble as an inevitable part of life, and when it comes, hold your head high, look it squarely in the eye and say, 'I will be bigger than you. You cannot defeat me.' Then repeat to yourself the most comforting words of all, 'This too will pass.'

Ann Landers, b. 1918
American advice columnist

Seek ye counsel of the aged, for their eyes have looked on the faces of the years and their ears have hearkened to the voices of Life. Even if their counsel is displeasing to you, pay heed to them.

Kahlil Gibran, 1883-1931
Lebanese poet, artist and mystic

When you can, always advise people to
do what you see they really want to do, so
long as what they want to do isn't dangerously
unlawful, stupidly unsocial or obviously
imposssible. Doing what they want to do,
they may succeed; doing what they don't
want to do, they won't.

James Gould Cozzens, 1903-1978
American writer

Do a little more than you're paid to;
Give a little more than you have to;
Try a little harder than you want to;
Aim a little higher than you think possible;
And give a lot of thanks to God for health,
family and friends.

Art Linkletter
American television personality

Consult your friend on all things, especially on
those which concern yourself. His counsel may
then be useful where your own self-love may
impair your judgement.

Seneca, c. 4 BC - 65 AD
Roman philosopher, dramatist, poet and statesman

Whenever you are asked if you can do a job, tell 'em, 'Certainly I can!' — and get busy and find out how to do it.

Theodore Roosevelt, 1858-1919
President of the United States of America

We have to steer our true life's course. Whatever your calling is in life! The whole purpose of being here is to figure out what that is as soon as possible, so you go about the business of being on track, of not being owned by what your mother said, what society said, whatever people think a woman is supposed to be . . . when you can exceed other people's expectations and be defined by your own!

Oprah Winfrey, b. 1954
American television personality

Generosity gives assistance rather than advice.

Marquis de Vauvenargues, 1715-1745
French soldier and writer

Ageing

Old age is not an illness, it is a timeless
ascent. As power diminishes, we grow
toward the light.

May Sarton, 1912-1995
American writer and poet

One should never count the years — one
should count one's interests. I have kept young
trying never to lose my childhood sense of
wonderment. I am glad I still have a vivid
curiosity about the world I live in.

Helen Keller, 1880-1968
Blind and deaf American writer and scholar

Wrinkles should merely indicate where smiles
have been.

Mark Twain, 1835-1910
American humorist and writer

Ageing is a life-spanning process of growth and development from birth to death. Old age is an integral part of the whole, bringing fulfilment and self-actualisation. I regard ageing as a triumph, a result of strength and survivorship.

Margaret Kuhn, b. 1905
American civil rights activist

I have no romantic feelings about age. Either you are interesting at any age or you are not. There is nothing particularly interesting about being old — or being young, for that matter.

Katharine Hepburn, b. 1907
American actress

There is nothing more liberating than age.

Liz Carpenter, b. 1920
American feminist writer

I am delighted to be with you. In fact, at my age, I am delighted to be anywhere.

Ronald Reagan, b. 1911
President of the United States of America

Thank God I have the seeing eye, that is to say, as I lie in bed I can walk step by step on the fells and rough land seeing every stone and flower and patch of bog and cotton pass where my old legs will never take me again.

Beatrix Potter, 1866-1943
British children's writer and illustrator

The wiser mind
Mourns less for what age takes away
Than what it leaves behind.

William Wordsworth, 1770-1850
English poet

It is quite wrong to think of old age as a downward slope. On the contrary, one climbs higher and higher with the advancing years, and that, too, with surprising strides. Brain-work comes as easily to the old as physical exertion to the child. One is moving, it is true, towards the end of life, but that end is now a goal, and not a reef in which the vessel may be dashed.

George Sand (Amandine Dupin) 1804-1876
French novelist

By the bye, as I must leave off being young, I find many Douceurs in being a sort of Chaperone for I am put on the Sofa near the fire and can drink as much wine as I like.

Jane Austen, 1775-1816
English novelist
From a letter to her sister Cassandra

I prefer to forget both pairs of glasses and spend my declining years saluting strange women and grandfather clocks.

Ogden Nash, 1902-1971
American humorous poet

Perhaps middle age is, or should be, a period of shedding shells: the shell of ambition, the shell of material accumulations and possessions, the shell of ego.

Anne Morrow Lindbergh, b. 1906
American writer

I am still not ready to accept completely grey hair. I try to keep fit — eat vegetarian meals, walk, swim and practise yoga. Mostly I accept my body as a record of my life.

Margaret Henry, b. 1934
Australian writer

I am 65 and I guess that puts me in with the geriatrics. But if there were 15 months in every year, I'd only be 48. That's the trouble with us. We number everything. Take women, for example, I think they deserve to have more than 12 years between the ages of 28 and 40.

James Thurber, 1894-1961
American writer and cartoonist

Our hearts are young 'neath wrinkled rind: life's more interesting than we thought.

Andrew Lang, 1844-1912
Scottish poet

When I passed the seventieth milestone ten months ago I instantly realised that I had entered a new country and a new atmosphere... I now believe that the best of life begins at seventy, for then your work is done; you know that you have done your best, let the quality of the work be what it may; that you have earned your holiday...and that henceforth to the setting of the sun nothing will break it, nothing interrupt it.

Mark Twain, 1835-1910
American humorist and writer

I gave my youth and beauty to men. I am going to give my wisdom and experience to animals.

Brigitte Bardot, b. 1934
French actress and animal rights campaigner

One of the signs of passing youth is the birth of a sense of fellowship with other human beings as we take our place among them.

Virginia Woolf, 1882-1941
English novelist

Becoming a grandmother is more often a middle-age than an old-age event. For many women today this is a time when, free of immediate family responsibilities, they discover new skills and at last are able to do what they want to do. The idea of old age is also changing. Women in their sixties and seventies do not get old. Instead we enter an active and satisfying 'third age', and after that, at eighty, a happy and contented 'fourth age'.

Sheila Kitzinger, b. 1929
Obstetrician and writer

Life has got to be lived — that's all there is to it. At seventy, I would say the advantage is that you take life more calmly. You know that 'this too will pass!'

Eleanor Roosevelt, 1884-1962
First Lady of the United States of America, writer and diplomat

Grow old along with me!
The best is yet to be.

Robert Browning, 1812-1889
English poet

The process of maturing is an art to be learned, an effort to be sustained. By the age of fifty you have made yourself what you are and, if it is good, it is better than your youth.

Marya Mannes, b. 1904
American journalist

Age puzzles me. I thought it was a quiet time. My seventies were interesting and fairly serene, but my eighties are passionate. I grow more intense as I age.

Florida Scott-Maxwell, 1883-1979
American-born English writer and psychologist

Age only matters when one is ageing. Now that I have arrived at a great age, I might as well be twenty.

Pablo Picasso, 1881-1973
Spanish painter and sculptor

Ambition

Ambition never gets anywhere until it forms a
partnership with work.

Anonymous

If you wish in this world to advance
Your merits you're bound to enhance,
You must stir it and stump it,
And blow your own trumpet
Or, trust me, you haven't a chance!

W. S. Gilbert, 1836-1911
English dramatist and librettist

The fellow who has an abundance of push gets
along very well without pull.

Anonymous

Anger

Anybody can become angry. That is not difficult; but to be angry with the right person and to the right degree, and at the right time, and for the right purpose, and in the right way: that is not within everybody's capability and it is not easy.

Aristotle, 384-322 BC
Greek philosopher

For every minute you remain angry you give up sixty seconds of peace of mind.

Ralph Waldo Emerson, 1803-1882
American essayist, poet and philosopher

Anger is short-lived in a good man.

Thomas Fuller, 1608-1661
English clergyman and writer

Animals

Love the animals: God has given them the rudiments of thought and joy untroubled.

Feodor Dostoevsky, 1821-1881
Russian writer

All animals except man know that the ultimate of life is to enjoy it.

Samuel Butler, 1835-1902
English writer

God made all the animals and gave
them our love and our fear,
To give sign, we and they are his children,
one family here.

Robert Browning, 1812-1889
English poet

Heaven goes by favour. If it went by merit, you would stay out and your dog would go in.

Mark Twain, 1835-1910
American humorist and writer

I think I could turn and live with animals,
they're so placid and self-contained. I stand
and look at them long and long.

Walt Whitman, 1819-1892
American poet and writer

Our perfect companions never have
fewer than four feet.

Colette, 1873-1954
French writer

I really don't think I could consent to
go to Heaven if I thought there were to
be no animals there.

George Bernard Shaw, 1856-1950
Irish writer, dramatist and critic

Apology

A man should never be ashamed to own
he has been in the wrong, which is but saying,
in other words, that he is wiser today
than he was yesterday.

Alexander Pope, 1688-1744
English poet

A true apology is more than just
acknowledgement of a mistake. It is
recognition that something you have said or
done has damaged a relationship and that you
care enough about the relationship to want it
repaired and restored.

Norman Vincent Peale, 1898-1993
American writer and minister

A sincere apology takes courage and humility.

Anonymous

Attitude

I've never been poor, only broke. Being poor
is a frame of mind. Being broke is only
a temporary setback.

Mike Todd, 1903-1958
American film producer

The greater part of our happiness or
misery depends on our dispositions and
not our circumstances.

Martha Washington, 1732-1802
First Lady of the United States of America

There is nothing either good or bad, but
thinking makes it so.

William Shakespeare, 1564-1616
English poet and playwright

I don't sing because I'm happy;
I'm happy because I sing.

William James, 1842-1910
American psychologist and philosopher

If, from time to time, we look at the blessings
in our lives, at the warmth and care and love
so many people respond with when there is a
tragedy, at the fact that we can walk and talk,
eat and breathe, then maybe we would re-
evaluate our bad moods and become aware
that all negative thoughts bring with them
more negativity, but all love shared
returns a thousandfold.
'As a man thinketh' perhaps best describes how
we are the creators of our own worlds.

Elisabeth Kübler-Ross, b. 1926
Swiss-born American psychiatrist

I always prefer to believe the best of
everybody; it saves so much trouble.

Rudyard Kipling, 1865-1936
Indian-born British poet and writer

Life appears to me too short to be spent in nursing animosity or registering wrong.

Charlotte Brontë, 1816-1855
British novelist

It is our attitude at the beginning of a difficult undertaking which, more than anything else, will determine its successful outcome.

William James, 1842-1910
American psychologist and philosopher

Nothing can hurt you unless you give it the power to do so.

A Course in Miracles

Authority

When you make peace with authority, you become authority.

Jim Morrison, 1943-1971
American rock singer

B

Balance

There are as many nights as days, and the one
is just as long as the other in the year's course.
Even a happy life cannot be without a measure
of darkness, and the word 'happy' would lose
its meaning if it were not balanced by sadness.
It is far better to take things as they come
along with patience and equanimity.

Carl Jung, 1875-1961
Swiss psychiatrist

Everyone is a moon and has a dark side which
he never shows to anybody.

Mark Twain, 1835-1910
American humorist and writer

To be a woman is to have interests and duties, raying out in all directions from the central mother-core, like spokes from the hub of a wheel . . . We must be open to all points of the compass; husband, children, friends, home, community; stretched out, exposed, like a spider's web to each breeze that blows, to each call that comes. How difficult for us, then, to achieve a balance in the midst of these contradictory tensions, and yet how necessary for the proper functioning of our lives.

Anne Morrow Lindbergh, b. 1906
American writer

Beauty

Beauty is the gift of God.

Aristotle, 384-322 BC
Greek philosopher

Cheerfulness and contentment are great beautifiers and are famous preservers of youthful good looks.

Charles Dickens, 1812-1870
English writer

Everything has its beauty but not
everyone sees it.

Confucius, c. 550-c. 478 BC
Chinese philosopher

Beauty is God's handwriting,
Welcome it
in every fair face,
every fair day,
every fair flower.

Charles Kingsley, 1819-1875
English writer, poet and clergyman

Beauty is no quality in things themselves;
it exists merely in the mind which
contemplates them; and each mind
perceives a different beauty.

David Hume, 1711-1776
Scottish philosopher and historian

Beginning

The distance doesn't matter; it is only
the first step that is difficult.

Marquise de Deffand, 1697-1780
French noblewoman

There is an old saying 'well begun is half done'
. . . I would use instead — Not begun at
all until half done.

John Keats, 1795-1821
English poet

The right moment for starting on your next job
is not tomorrow or next week; it is *instanter*,
or in the American idiom, right now.

Arnold Toynbee, 1899-1975
English historian

Belief

Believe you can, and you can. Belief is one of the most powerful of all problem dissolvers. When you believe that a difficulty can be overcome, you are more than halfway to victory over it already.

Norman Vincent Peale, 1898-1993
American writer and minister

I believe in one God and no more, and I hope for happiness beyond this life. I believe in the equality of man; and I believe that religious duties consist in doing justice, loving mercy and in endeavouring to make our fellow creatures happy.

Thomas Paine, 1737-1809
English-born American revolutionary philosopher and writer

No one of you is a believer until he desires for his brother that which he desires for himself.

Islamic spirituality

Best

I do the very best I know how — the very best I can; and I mean to keep on doing it until the end.

Abraham Lincoln, 1809-1865
American statesman and President

When we do the best we can, we never know what miracle is wrought in our life, or the life of another.

Helen Keller, 1880-1968
Blind and deaf American writer and scholar

I have tried simply to write the best I can; sometimes I have good luck and write better than I can.

Ernest Hemingway, 1898-1961
American writer

Blessings

Let there be many windows in your soul,
That all the glories of the universe
May beautify it.

Ralph Waldo Trine, 1866-1958
American poet and writer

Bless the four corners of this little house
And be the lintel blessed;
And bless the hearth, and bless the board
And bless each place of rest.

Anonymous

Reflect on your present blessings, of
which every man has many, not on your past
misfortunes, of which all men have some.

Charles Dickens, 1812-1870
English writer

Books

No entertainment is so cheap as reading,
nor any pleasure so lasting.

Lady Mary Wortley Montague, 1689-1762
English poet and writer

Then I thought of reading — the nice and
subtle happiness of reading . . . this joy not
dulled by age, this polite and unpunishable
vice, this selfish, serene, lifelong intoxication.

Logan Pearsall Smith, 1865-1946
American essayist

A good book is the precious lifeblood of a
master spirit, embalmed and treasured up on
purpose to a life beyond life.

John Milton, 1608-1674
English poet

A library is thought in cold storage.

Herbert Samuel, 1870-1963
British statesman

For books are more than books,
they are the life
The very heart and core of ages past,
The reason why men lived and
worked and died,
The essence and quintessence of their lives.

Amy Lowell, 1874-1925
American poet and writer

Study has been for me the sovereign remedy
against all the disappointments of life. I have
never known any trouble that an hour's
reading would not dissipate.

Charles Louis de Montesquieu, 1689-1755
French political philosopher

Books are the legacies that a great genius leaves
to mankind, which are delivered down from
generation to generation as presents to the
posterity of those who are not yet born.

Joseph Addison, 1672-1719
English essayist

The books read in childhood . . . create in one's mind a sort of false map of the world, a series of fabulous countries into which one can retreat at odd moments throughout the rest of life, and which in some cases can even survive a visit to the real countries which they are supposed to represent.

George Orwell, 1903-1950
English novelist and essayist

Books, books, books. It was not that I read so much. I read and re-read the same ones. But all of them were necessary to me. Their presence, their smell, the letters of their titles, and the texture of their leather bindings.

Colette, 1873-1954
French writer

We read books to find out who we are. What other people, real or imaginary, do and think and feel is an essential guide to our understanding of what we ourselves are and may become.

Ursula LeGuin, b. 1929
American science fiction writer

The best effect of any book is that it excites
the reader to self activity.

Thomas Carlyle, 1875-1881
Scottish historian, essayist and critic

My early and invincible love of reading I
would not exchange for all the riches of India.

Edward Gibbon, 1737-1794
British historian

You may have tangible wealth untold,
Caskets of jewels and coffers of gold.
Richer than I you can never be —
I had a mother who read to me.

Strickland Gillilan, 1869-1954
Writer and poet

Mankind would lose half its wisdom built up
over the centuries if it lost its great sayings.
They contain the best parts of the best books.

Thomas Jefferson, 1743-1826
President of the United States of America

No furniture so charming as books, even if you never open them, or read a single word.

Sydney Smith, 1771-1845
English clergyman, essayist and wit

. . . books, because of their weight and texture, and because of their sweetly token resistance to manipulation, involve our hands and eyes, and then our minds and souls, in a spiritual adventure I would be very sorry for my grandchildren not to know about.

Kurt Vonnegut, b. 1922
American novelist

When I am attacked by gloomy thoughts, nothing helps me so much as running to my books. They quickly absorb me and banish the clouds from my mind.

Michel de Montaigne, 1533-1592
French essayist

Boredom

Life is so full of exciting things to do and see that we should never be bored. Watch the sunrise from a hot-air balloon, go swimming with dolphins, take up bushwalking, join a book club, learn a foreign language. Try out at least one new and interesting thing each year.

Anonymous

There is no such thing as an uninteresting subject; the only thing that can exist is an uninterested person.

G. K. Chesterton, 1874-1936
English writer and critic

Is not life a hundred times too short for us to bore ourselves?

Friedrich Nietzsche, 1844-1900
German philosopher

C

Challenges

If you continuously face challenges,
one of two things can happen:
You either collapse under the strain, lose
confidence in your ability and walk away
defeated — perhaps to fight again later or to
just drift into a life of non-challenge. Or you
win a few impossibles and are then encouraged
to have a go at the next impossible. So that
before long, you find the impossibles have
become possible.

Sara Henderson, B. 1936
Australian outback station manager and writer

There are no problems — only challenges.

Anonymous

Change

Keep in mind in how many things you yourself have already seen change. The universe is change. Life is understanding.

Marcus Aurelius, 121-180 AD
Roman emperor and philosopher

Life is change. Growth is optional. Choose wisely.

Karen Kaiser Clark, b. 1938
American legislator and feminist

We must always change, renew, rejuvenate ourselves; otherwise we harden.

Johann von Goethe, 1749-1832
German writer, dramatist and scientist

Learn to adapt, adjust and accommodate.

Sai Baba
Indian spiritual master

If you don't like the way the world is, you change it. You have an obligation to change it. You just do it one step at a time.

Marian Wright Edelman, b. 1937
American attorney and civil rights activist

The foolish and the dead alone never change their opinions.

James Russell Lowell, 1819-1891
American poet and diplomat

To live is to change, and to be perfect is to have changed often.

Cardinal John Henry Newman, 1801-1890
English theologian and writer

There is no sin punished more implacably by nature than the sin of resistance to change.

Anne Morrow Lindbergh, b. 1906
American writer

Only the wisest and stupidest of men
never change.

Confucius, c. 550-c. 478 BC
Chinese philosopher

If you are not happy with yourself, make a
conscious effort to change whatever it is you
don't like. It is never too late to become a
better, more caring person.

Anonymous

Let us never confuse stability with stagnation.

Mary Jean LeTendre, b. 1948
American educator

Progress is impossible without change; and
those who cannot change their minds cannot
change anything.

George Bernard Shaw, 1856-1950
Irish dramatist, writer and critic

Character

I desire so to conduct the affairs of this administration that if at the end, when I come to lay down the reins of power, I have lost every other friend on earth, I shall at least have one friend left, and that friend shall be down inside of me.

Abraham Lincoln, 1809-1865
American statesman and President

The strongest man in the world is the man who stands alone.

Henrik Ibsen, 1828-1906
Norwegian writer, dramatist and poet

Character-building begins in our infancy and continues until death.

Eleanor Roosevelt, 1884-1962
First Lady of the United States of America, writer and diplomat

Character cannot be developed in ease and quiet. Only through experience of trial and suffering can the soul be strengthened, vision cleared, ambition inspired and success achieved.

Helen Keller, 1880-1968
Blind and deaf American writer and scholar

The best index to a person's character is how he treats people who can't do him any good, and how he treats people who can't fight back.

Abigail Van Buren, b. 1918
American advice columnist

It is easy in the world to live after the world's opinions. It is easy in solitude to live after our own; but the great man is he who, in the midst of the crowd, keeps with perfect sweetness the independence of solitude.

Ralph Waldo Emerson, 1803-1882
American essayist, poet and philosopher

Children & Parents

Of all the joys that brighten suffering earth,
What joy is welcom'd like a newborn child!

Caroline Norton, 1808-1877
Irish writer and reformer

Every child born into the world is a
new thought of God, an ever fresh and
radiant possibility.

Kate Douglas Wiggin, 1856-1923
American writer and educator

Children are an affirmation of life itself. They
have shown me how much fun it is to simply
enjoy nature; the sea even when the water is
freezing, the stars which twinkle and hint at
life beyound ourselves, the earth which
squishes and squelches in my hands,
these are things I enjoy again.

Susan Bourke
Australian writer

God sent childen for another purpose than merely to keep up the race — to enlarge our hearts; and to make us unselfish and full of kindly sympathies and affections; to give our souls higher aims; to call out all our faculties to extended enterprise and exertion; and to bring round our firesides bright faces, happy smiles and loving, tender hearts.

Mary Botham Howitt, 1799-1888
English author

The soul is healed by being with children.

Feodor Dostoevsky, 1821-1881
Russian writer

To talk to a child, to fascinate him, is much more difficult than to win an electoral victory. But it is more rewarding.

Colette, 1873-1954
French writer

It's always been my feeling that God lends you your children until they're about eighteen years old. If you haven't made your points with them by then, it's too late.

Betty Ford, b. 1918
First Lady of the United States of America

We should say to each of them: Do you know what you are? You are a marvel. You are unique . . . You may become a Shakespeare, a Michelangelo, a Beethoven. You have the capacity for anything . . .

Pablo Casals, 1876-1973
Spanish cellist, conductor and composer

What good mothers and fathers instinctively feel like doing for their babies is usually best after all.

Benjamin Spock, 1903-1998
American paediatrician

You are the bows from which your
children as living arrows are sent forth.
The Archer sees the mark upon the path
of the infinite,
And He bends you with His might that
His arrows may go swift and far.
Let your bending in the Archer's
hand be for gladness;
For even as He loves the arrow that flies,
so He loves the bow that is stable.

Kahlil Gibran, 1883-1931
Lebanese poet, artist and mystic

I think it must be written somewhere that
the virtues of the mother shall be
visited on the children.

Charles Dickens, 1812-1870
English novelist

My mother was the making of me. She was
so true, so sure of me, and I felt that
I had someone to live for; someone
I must not disappoint.

Thomas Edison, 1847-1931
American inventor

All that I am or hope to be,
I owe to my mother.

Abraham Lincoln, 1809-1865
American statesman and President

My mother had a great deal of trouble with
me, but I think she enjoyed it.

Mark Twain, 1835-1910
American humorist and writer

Mother is the name for God in the lips and
hearts of little children.

William Makepeace Thackeray, 1811-1863
English writer

The mother's heart is the child's school room.

Henry Beecher Ward, 1818-1887
American clergyman and writer

To bring up a child in the way he should go,
travel that way yourself once in a while.

Josh Billings, 1818-1885
American humorist

If a child lives with approval,
He learns to like himself.

Dorothy Law Nolte
American poet

There are two lasting legacies we can
hope to give to our children. One of
these is roots; the other, wings.

Anonymous

When I was a boy of fourteen, my father was
so ignorant I could hardly stand to have the old
man around. But when I got to be twenty-one,
I was astonished at how much he had learned
in seven years.

Mark Twain, 1835-1910
American humorist and writer

I'm doing this for my father. I'm quite happy
that they see me as my father's daughter. My
only concern is that I prove worthy of him.

Aung San Suu Kyi, b. 1945
*Burma's democratically elected leader,
winner of Nobel Peace Prize and daughter of
Burma's hero Aung San*

Choice

You don't get to choose how you're going
to die. Or when. You can decide how
you're going to live now.

Joan Baez, b. 1941
American folksinger

Choice, not chance, determines destiny.

Anonymous

Few people make a deliberate choice between
good and evil; the choice is between what we
want to do and what we ought to do.

Anonymous

In any moment of decision, the best thing
you can do is the right thing, the next best
thing is the wrong thing, and the worst
thing is to do nothing.

Theodore Roosevelt, 1858-1919
President of the United States of America

He who deliberates at length before taking a
single step will spend his whole life on one leg.

Chinese proverb

Civility

A drop of honey catches more flies
than a gallon of gall.

Abraham Lincoln, 1809-1865
American statesman and President

Civility costs nothing and buys everything.

Lady Mary Wortley Montague, 1689-1762
British poet and writer

If a man is gracious and courteous to strangers,
it shows he is a citizen of the world.

Francis Bacon, 1561-1626
British philosopher, essayist and courtier

The great secret, Eliza, is not having bad
manners or good manners, or any particular
sort of manners, but having the same
manner for all human souls . . .

George Bernard Shaw, 1856-1950
Irish dramatist, writer and critic

[Pygmalion]

They say courtesy is contagious.
So why not start an epidemic?

Anonymous

Punctuality is the politeness of kings.

Louis XV111, 1755-1824
King of France

Comforting Words

Master, what is the best way to
meet the loss of someone we love?
By knowing that when we truly love, it is never lost. It is only after death that the depth of the bond is truly felt, and our loved one becomes more a part of us than was possible in life.

Oriental tradition

Do but consider, however, if we live apart, as we must, it is much the same whether I am hundreds or thousands of miles distant from you. The same Providence will watch over us there as here. The sun that shines on you will also afford me the benefit of its cheering rays.

Elizabeth Macarthur, 1767-1850
English-born wife of John Macarthur, founder of
the Australian wool industry, in a letter to her
mother in England

And remember, we all stumble,
every one of us. That's why it's a
comfort to go hand in hand.

E. K. Brough
American writer

For the winter is past,
the rain is over and gone.
The flowers are springing up and the time
of the singing of the birds has come.
Yes, spring is here.

Song of Solomon 2: 11-12

Communication

Starting with self-communication in
private, you can then develop your ability
to communicate with others. Being clear
with yourself opens the way for being
more clear with others about how you
feel and think, enriching your relationships
and social interactions.

Lucia Capacchione
American art therapist and pioneer in inner healing

Use what language you will, you can never say anything to others but what you are.

Ralph Waldo Emerson, 1803-1882
American essayist, poet and philosopher

Only connect!

E. M. Forster, 1879-1970
English novelist

How wonderful it is to say the right thing at the right time. A good man thinks before he speaks; the evil man pours out his evil words without a thought.

Proverbs 15:23, 28

Give every man thy ear, but few thy voice.

William Shakespeare, 1564-1616
English playwright and poet

Speaking without thinking is like shooting without taking aim.

Spanish proverb

Compassion

Compassion is not a sloppy, sentimental feeling for people who are underprivileged or sick . . . it is an absolutely practical belief that, regardless of a person's background, ability or ability to pay, he should be provided with the best that society has to offer.

Neil Kinnock. b. 1942
Welsh politician

When a man has pity on all living creatures then only is he noble.

Buddha, c. 563-483 BC
Indian religious leader and founder of Buddhism

By compassion we make others' misery our own, and so, by relieving them, we relieve ourselves also.

Thomas Browne, 1605-1682
English author and physician

Conscience

The one thing that doesn't abide by majority
rule is a person's conscience.

Harper Lee, b. 1926
American novelist

A good conscience is a soft pillow.

German proverb

Keep pace with the drummer you hear,
however measured or far away.

Henry David Thoreau, 1817-1862
American essayist, poet and mystic

The voice of conscience is so delicate that
it is easy to stifle it: but it is also so clear
that it is impossible to mistake it.

Mme Anne de Staël, 1766-1817
Swiss-born French writer

Better to stand ten thousand sneers than
one abiding pang, such as time could
not abolish, of bitter self-reproach.

Thomas de Quincey, 1785-1859
English essayist

Some good must come by clinging to the
right. Conscience is a man's compass, and
though the needle sometimes deviates,
though one perceives irregularities in
directing one's course by it, still one
must try to follow its direction.

Vincent Van Gogh, 1853-1890
Dutch post-impressionist painter

He that loses his conscience has nothing left
that is worth keeping.

Isaak Walton, 1593-1683
English writer

A peace above all earthly dignities,
A still and quiet conscience.

William Shakespeare, 1564-1616
English playwright and poet

Contentment

To be content, look backward on those who possess less than yourself, not forward on those who possess more.

Benjamin Franklin, 1706-1790
American statesman and scientist

A person who is not disturbed by the incessant flow of desires can alone achieve peace, and not the man who strives to satisfy such desires.

Bhagavad Gita

Health is the greatest gift, contentment the greatest wealth, faithfulness the best relationship.

Buddha. c. 563-483 BC
Indian religious leader, founder of Buddhism

He is richest who is content with the least, for content is the wealth of nature.

Socrates, 468-399 BC
Greek philosopher

Conversation

Conversation. What is it? A mystery! It's the art of never seeming bored, of touching everything with interest, of pleasing with trifles, of being fascinating with nothing at all. How do we define this lively darting about with words, of hitting them back and forth, this short brief smile of ideas which should be conversation?

Guy de Maupassant, 1850-1893
French writer

Ideal conversation must be an exchange of thought, and not, as many of those who worry most about their shortcomings believe, an eloquent exhibition of wit or oratory.

Emily Post, 1873-1960
American etiquette writer

Good nature is more agreeable in conversation than wit and gives a certain air to the counte-nance which is more amiable than beauty.

Joseph Addison, 1672-1719
English essayist

Conversation has a kind of charm about it, an insinuating and insidious something that elicits secrets from us just like love or liquor.

Seneca, c. 4 BC-65 AD
Roman philosopher, dramatist, poet and statesman

For one word a man is often declared to be wise, and for one word he can be judged to be foolish. We should be careful indeed what we say.

Confucius, c. 550-c. 478 BC
Chinese philosopher

That is the happiest conversation where there is no competition, no vanity, but a calm quiet interchange of sentiments.

Samuel Johnson, 1709-1784
English lexicographer, essayist and wit

Courage

I am not afraid of storms for I am
learning to sail my ship.

Louisa May Alcott, 1832-1888
American novelist

Life shrinks or expands in proportion
to one's courage.

Anaïs Nin, 1903-1977
French novelist

Fearlessness may be a gift, but perhaps
more precious is the courage acquired through
endeavour, courage that come from cultivating
the habit of refusing to let fear dictate one's
actions, courage that could be described as
'grace under pressure' — grace which is
renewed repeatedly in the face of harsh,
unremitting pressure.

Aung San Suu Kyi, b. 1945
*Burma's democratically elected leader and winner of
Nobel Peace Prize*

Courage is the price that life
   extracts for granting peace.
The soul that knows it not, knows
   no release
From little things,
Knows not the livid loneliness of fear
Nor mountain heights where
   bitter joy can hear
The sound of wings.

Amelia Earhart, 1898-1937
American aviator

A light supper, a good night's sleep, and
a fine morning have sometimes made a hero
of the same man who, by an indigestion, a
restless night and a rainy morning, would
have proved a coward.

Lord Chesterfield, 1694-1773
English statesman

Never bend your head, always hold it high.
Look the world in the face.

Helen Keller, 1880-1968
Blind and deaf American writer and scholar

I wanted you to see what real courage is, instead of getting the idea that courage is a man with a gun in his hand. It's when you know you're licked before you begin but you begin anyway and you see it through no matter what.

Harper Lee, b. 1926
American novelist

My message to you is:
Be courageous!
Be as brave as your fathers before you.
Have faith!
Go forward.

Thomas Edison, 1847-1931
American inventor

Facing it, always facing it, that's the way to get through. Face it.

Joseph Conrad, 1856-1924
Polish-born British writer

Courage faces fear and thereby masters it.
Cowardice represses fear and is thereby
mastered by it.

Martin Luther King, Jr, 1929-1968
American civil rights leader and minister

It's better to be a lion for a day than
a sheep all your life.

Sister Elizabeth Kenny, 1866-1952
Australian nurse and pioneer in polio treatment

I hate a fellow whom pride, or cowardice, or
laziness drives into a corner, and who does
nothing when he is there but sit and growl;
let him come out as I do, and bark.

Samuel Johnson, 1709-1784
English lexicographer, essayist and wit

The bravest thing you can do when you are not
brave is to profess courage and act accordingly.

Corra May White Harris, 1869-1935
American writer

No coward soul is mine,
No trembler in the world's
  storm-troubled sphere;
I see Heaven's glory shine,
And faith shines equal, arming
  me from fear.

Emily Brontë,1818-1848
British novelist and poet

Strength alone knows courage. Weakness is below even defeat, and is born vanquished.

Anne Sophie Swetchine, 1782-1857
Russian writer

I count he braver who overcomes his desires than he who overcomes his enemies.

Aristotle, 384-322 BC
Greek philosopher

Creativity

No matter how old you get, if you can keep the desire to be creative, you're keeping the man-child alive.

John Cassavetes
American film director

In every real man a child is hidden who wants to play.

Friedrich Nietzche, 1844-1900
German philosopher

Art is an essential reminder of what it is in life that lasts, of why one lives. Art communicates, celebrates, mourns and remembers. What else in our lives can do this?

Bella Lewitzky, b. 1916
American ballet dancer

Poetry ennobles the heart and the eyes,
and unveils the meaning of all things upon
which the heart and the eyes dwell. It discovers
the secret rays of the universe, and restores
us to forgotten paradises.

Dame Edith Sitwell, 1887-1964
English poet

Masterpieces are not single and solitary births;
they are the outcome of many years of thinking
in common, of thinking by the body of
the people, so that the experience of the
mass is behind the single voice.

Virginia Woolf, 1882-1941
English novelist

Creativity is so delicate a flower that praise
tends to make it bloom, while discouragement
often nips it in the bud. Any of us will put
out more and better ideas if our efforts
are appreciated.

Alex F. Osborn, 1888-1966
American advertising director and writer

Crisis

The English word 'crisis' is translated by the Chinese by two little characters; one means 'danger' and the other means 'opportunity'.

Anonymous

Granted that we face a world crisis which often leaves us standing amid the surging murmur of life's restless sea. But every crisis has both its dangers and its opportunities. Each can spell either salvation or doom. In a dark, confused world the spirit of God may yet reign supreme.

Martin Luther King, Jr, 1929-1968
American civil rights leader and minister

Criticism

A true critic ought to dwell upon excellencies
rather than imperfections.

Joseph Addison, 1672-1719
English essayist

There is nothing as easy as denouncing. It don't
take much to see that something is wrong, but
it does take some eyesight to see what will put
it right again.

Will Rogers, 1879-1935
American humorist and writer

Don't find fault. Find a remedy.

Henry Ford, 1863-1947
American car manufacturer

Deal with the faults of others as gently
as your own.

Chinese proverb

Crying

I have always felt sorry for people afraid
of feeling, of sentimentality, who are unable
to weep with their whole heart. Because
those who do not know how to weep do not
know how to laugh either.

Golda Meir, 1898-1978
Prime Minister of Israel

We need never be ashamed of our tears.

Charles Dickens, 1812-1870
English writer

'It opens the lungs, washes the countenance,
exercises the eyes, and softens down the
temper,' said Mr Bumble. 'So cry away.'

Charles Dickens, 1812-1870
[Oliver Twist]

Curiosity

Curiosity will conquer fear even more
than bravery will.

James Stephens, 1882-1950
Irish novelist

Curiosity is the key to creativity.

Akio Morita
Japanese businessman

Curiosity has its own reason for existing . . .
Never lose a holy curiosity.

Albert Einstein, 1877-1955
German-born American physicist

Disinterested intellectual curiosity is the life
blood of real civilisation.

George Macaulay Trevelyan, 1876-1962
British historian

A generous and elevated mind is distinguished
by nothing more certainly than an eminent
degree of curiosity.

Samuel Johnson, 1709-1784
English lexicographer, essayist and wit

Curiosity is nothing more than freewheeling
intelligence.

Anonymous

Those with a lively sense of curiosity learn
something new every day of their lives.

Anonymous

D

Death

I think of death as some delightful journey
That I shall take when my tasks are done.

Ella Wheeler Wilcox, 1850-1919
American writer and poet

We sometimes congratulate ourselves at the
moment of waking from a troubled dream; it
may be so the moment after death.

Nathaniel Hawthorne, 1804-1864
American writer

Life is a great surprise. I do not see why death
should not be an even greater one.

Vladimir Nabokov, 1899-1977
Russian-born American novelist

The dead don't die. They look on and help.

D. H. Lawrence, 1855-1930
English writer and poet

Life does not cease to be funny when people die any more than it ceases to be serious when people laugh.

George Bernard Shaw, 1856-1950
Irish dramatist, writer and critic

There is no need to be afraid of death. It is not the end of the physical body that should worry us. Rather, our concern must be to live while we're alive — to release our inner selves from the spiritual death that comes from living behind a facade designed to conform to external definitions of who and what we are.

Elisabeth Kübler-Ross, b. 1926
Swiss-born American psychiatrist and writer

The world is the land of the dying; the next is the land of the living.

Tyron Edwards, 1809-1894
American theologian

You would know the secret of death.
But how shall you find it unless you seek
it in the heart of life?
The owl whose night-bound eyes are blind unto
the day cannot unveil the mystery of light.
If you would indeed behold the spirit of death,
open your heart wide unto the body of life.
For life and death are one,
even as river and sea are one.

Kahlil Gibran, 1883-1931
Lebanese poet, artist and mystic

The gods conceal from men the happiness of
death, that they may endure life.

Lucan, 39-65 AD
Roman poet

Depression

We can be cured of depression in only fourteen days if every day we will try to think of how we can be helpful to others.

Alfred Adler, 1870-1937
Austrian psychiatrist

The best way to cheer yourself up is to cheer someone else up.

Mark Twain, 1835-1910
American humorist and writer

Never give way to melancholy; resist it steadily, for the habit will encroach.

Sydney Smith, 1771-1845
English clergyman essayist and wit

Difficulties

Nothing is easy to the unwilling.

Thomas Fuller, 1608-1661
English clergyman and writer

The difficulties of life are meant to make us
better, not bitter.

Anonymous

Tackle any difficulty at first sight because the
longer you leave it the larger it grows.

Anonymous

Do what is easy as if it were difficult,
and what is difficult as if it were easy.

Baltasar Gracian, 1601-1658
Spanish writer and priest

Disappointment

Disappointment should be cremated, not embalmed.

Henry S. Haskins
American writer

Disappointment is often the salt of life.

Theodore Parker, 1810-1860
American Unitarian minister

Wisdom comes by disillusionment.

George Santayana, 1863-1952
Spanish philosopher and writer

Nothing worthwhile is achieved without patience, labour and disappointment.

Anonymous

Doubt

If a man will begin with certainties, he shall end in doubts. But if he will be content to begin with doubts, he shall end in certainties.

Francis Bacon, 1561-1626
British philosopher, essayist and courtier

Doubt is often the beginning of wisdom.

M. Scott Peck, b. 1936
American psychiatrist and writer

Doubt is an incitation to think.

Anonymous

Dreams

Always live your life with one more dream to fulfil. No matter how many of your dreams you have realised in the past, always have a dream to go. Because when you stop dreaming, life becomes a mundane existence.

Sara Henderson, b. 1936
Australian outback station manager and writer

It seems to me we can never give up longing and wishing while we are thoroughly alive. There are certain things we feel to be beautiful and good, and we must hunger after them.

George Eliot (Mary Ann Evans), 1819-1880
English novelist

I like the dreams of the future better than the history of the past.

Thomas Jefferson, 1743-1826
President of the United States of America

E

Education

Learning . . . should be a joy and full of excitement. It is life's greatest adventure; it is an illustrated excursion into the minds of noble and learned men, not a conducted tour through a jail.

Taylor Caldwell, 1900-1985
American writer

The roots of education are bitter, but the fruit is sweet.

Aristotle, 384-322 BC
Greek philosopher

Give a man a fish and you feed him for a day. Teach a man to fish and you feed him for a lifetime.

Chinese proverb

Learning is the only wealth tyrants cannot despoil. Only death can dim the lamp of knowledge that is within you. The true wealth of a nation lies not in its gold or silver but in its learning, wisdom and in the uprightness of its sons.

Kahlil Gibran, 1883-1931
Lebanese poet, artist and mystic

If a man empties his purse into his head, no one can take it from him.

Benjamin Franklin, 1706-1790
American statesman and scientist

For as the old saying is,
When house and land are gone and spent
Then learning is most excellent.

Samuel Foote, 1720-1777
English actor, dramatist and wit

Train a child in the way he should go, and when he is old he will not depart from it.

Proverbs, 12:4

The primary purpose of a liberal education is to make one's mind a pleasant place in which to spend one's leisure.

Sydney J. Harris, b. 1911
American journalist

The supreme end of education is expert discernment in all things — the power to tell the good from the bad, the genuine from the counterfeit, and to prefer the good and genuine to the bad and counterfeit.

Samuel Johnson, 1709-1784
English lexicographer, essayist and wit

What you teach your children is what you *really* believe in.

Cathy Warner Weatherford, b. 1951
American educator

Education should be gentle and stern, not cold and lax.

Joseph Joubert, 1754-1824
French writer and moralist

Effort

I loathe drudgery as much as any man, but I
have learned that the only way to conquer
drudgery is to get through it as neatly, as
efficiently, as one can. You know perfectly well
that a dull job slackly done becomes twice as
dull; whereas a dull job which you try to do
just as well as you can becomes half as dull.
Here again, effort appears to me the
main art of living.

Harold Nicolson, 1886-1968
Diplomat, politician, writer and diarist

It takes less time to do a thing right than it
does to explain why you did it wrong.

Henry Wadsworth Longfellow, 1807-1882
American poet and writer

Whatever is worth doing is worth doing well.

Lord Chesterfield, 1694-1773
English statesman

Empowerment

My will shall shape my future. Whether I fail or succeed shall be no man's doing but my own. I am the force. I can clear any obstacle before me or I can be lost in the maze. My choice; my responsibility; win or lose, only I hold the key to my destiny.

Elaine Maxwell
American writer

It isn't until you come to a spiritual understanding of who you are — not necessarily a religious feeling, but deep down, the spirit within — that you can begin to take control.

Oprah Winfrey, b. 1954
American television personality

Most powerful is he who has control over himself.

Seneca, 4 BC- AD 65
Roman philosopher, dramatist, poet and statesman

Never doubt that a small group of thoughtful
committed citizens can change the world.
Indeed, it is the only thing that ever has.

Margaret Mead, 1901-1978
American anthropologist and writer

One oral utterance, which boldly states
how you want your life to be, is worth more
than a dozen books read or lectures attended.
Spoken words describing the good you want,
help you to claim it and release it into your
own life quickly.

Catherine Ponder
American motivational writer

I am only one; but still I am one. I cannot do
everything, but still I can do something; I will
not refuse to do the something I can do.

Helen Keller, 1880-1968
Blind and deaf American writer and scholar

Encouragement

Correction does much but encouragement
does more.

Johann von Goethe, 1749-1832
German writer, dramatist and scientist

It must be tempting to succumb to what I call
the FUD factor. I know because I've been
there. The Fear, Uncertainty and Doubt is only
put there by the detractors and critics who
don't know you anyway. You are there because
you are the best and they are not, remember
that. I know you will ignore the distractions.
FOCUS on the job at hand, and
CONCENTRATE on yours and the team's
GOALS (in that order). You will succeed
because you have what it takes . . .

Kieren Perkins, b. 1973
Australian Olympic swimming gold medallist
From a fax in June 1997 to Mark Taylor, Australian
cricket captain 1994-1999

I don't blame the system for my mistakes,
I blame myself . . . Right now I'm being
offered six potentially wonderful pictures. I
think I'm a good example for anyone who
thinks their situation is hopeless. Keep putting
one foot in front of the other, keep showing
up, and you can turn it around.

John Frankenheimer
American film director

Encouragement is like premium gasoline. It
helps to take the knock out of living.

Anonymous

A few words of encouragement can
sometimes tip the scales between another's
failure or success.

Anonymous

Enjoyment

Our wealth lies not in what we have
but in what we enjoy.

Anonymous

True enjoyment comes from activity of
the mind and exercise of the body; the two
are ever united.

Alexander von Humboldt, 1769-1859
German statesman, naturalist and writer

Why not learn to enjoy the little things?
There are so many of them.

Anonymous

I spent most of my money on wine, women
and fast cars – and wasted the rest.

Josh Gaspero
American publisher

Enthusiasm

Every great and commanding movement in the annals of the world is a triumph of enthusiasm.

Ralph Waldo Emerson. 1803-1882
American essayist, poet and philosopher

You must learn day by day, year by year, to broaden your horizon. The more things you love, the more you are interested in, the more you enjoy, the more you are indignant about, the more you have left when anything happens.

Ethel Barrymore, 1879-1959
American actress

If it were as easy to arouse enthusiasm as it is suspicion, just think what could be accomplished.

Anonymous

You can do anything if you have enthusiasm.
Enthusiasm is the yeast that makes your
hopes rise to the stars. Enthusiasm is the
spark in your eye, the swing in your gait, the
grip of your hand, the irresistible surge of
your will and your energy to execute your
ideas. Enthusiasts are fighters, they have
fortitude, they have staying qualities.
Enthusiasm is at the bottom of all progress!
With it, there is accomplishment.
Without it, there are only alibis.

Henry Ford, 1863-1947
American car manufacturer

We could hardly wait to get up in the morning!

Wilbur Wright, 1867-1912 and
Orville Wright , 1871-1948
American inventors

Just don't give up trying what you really want
to do. Where there is love and inspiration, I
don't think you can go wrong.

Ella Fitzgerald, 1918-1996
American singer

Let your enthusiasm radiate in your voice, your actions, your facial expressions, your personality, the words you use, and the thoughts you think! Nothing great was ever achieved without enthusiasm.

Ralph Waldo Emerson, 1803-1882
American essayist, poet and philosopher

Love the moment, and the energy of that moment will spread beyond all boundaries.

Corita Kent, b. 1918
American graphic artist

Nothing is so contagious as enthusiasm . . . It is the genius of sincerity and truth accomplishes no victories without it.

Edward Bulwer-Lytton, 1803-1873
British novelist and politician

Epitaphs

She would rather light a candle than curse the darkness, and her glow has warmed the earth.

Adlai Stevenson, 1900-1965
*American lawyer, statesman and
United Nations ambassador*

[Written on the death of Eleanor Roosevelt]

The friend of man, the friend of truth;
The friend of age, the guide of youth;
If there's another world, he lives in bliss;
If there is none, he made the best of this.

Robert Burns, 1759-1796
Scottish poet

[Epistle to the Rev. John McMath]

You could write a list of epitaphs which describe a perfect life. They describe Peter's [Peter Cook's] perfectly.

1. He added to the sum of human happiness.
2. He never harmed anyone but himself.
3. He left the world a better place than he found it.
4. He never achieved anything at the expense of anyone else.
5. He made innumerable friends, but not one enemy.
6. He never complained.
7. He was never mean, boastful, envious or vain.
8. He never told anyone else how to behave.
9. He never betrayed a confidence.
10. He made people laugh.

God bless him.

Stephen Fry, b. 1947
English actor, comedian and writer

[Peter Cook Remembered]

Error

Truth emerges more readily from error than from confusion.

Francis Bacon, 1561-1626
British philosopher, essayist and courtier

Things could be worse. Suppose your errors were counted and published every day like those of a baseball player.

Anonymous

Great services are not cancelled by one act or by one single errror.

Benjamin Disraeli, 1804-1881
British Prime Minister and writer

An error doesn't become a mistake until you refuse to correct it.

Anonymous

Excellence

The secret of joy in work is contained in
one word — excellence. To know how to do
something well is to enjoy it.

Pearl S. Buck, 1892-1972
American writer and missionary

Excuses

Excuses fool no one but the person
who makes them.

Anonymous

The man who really wants to do something
finds a way; the other man makes an excuse.

Anonymous

Experience

The best advice you'll get is from someone who
has made the same mistake himself.

Anonymous

Experience is the child of Thought, and
Thought is the child of Action.

Benjamin Disraeli, 1804-1881
British Prime Minister and writer

There are many truths of which the full
meaning cannot be realised until personal
experience has brought it home.

John Stuart Mill, 1806-1873
English philosopher, reformer and politician

Experience is the wisdom that enables
us to recognise the folly that we have
already embraced.

Ambrose Bierce, 1842-1914
American journalist

We should be careful to get out of experience only the wisdom that is in it — and stop there; lest we be like the cat that sits down on the stove-lid. She will never sit down on a hot stove-lid again — and that is well; but also she will never sit down on a cold one anymore.

Mark Twain, 1835-1910
American humorist and writer

Experience is a good teacher, but she sends in terrific bills.

Minna Antrim, 1861-1950
American writer

The least expensive education is to learn from the mistakes of others.

Anonymous

F

Failure

The difference between failure and success
is doing a thing nearly right and doing
a thing exactly right.

Anonymous

Our greatest glory is not in never falling, but in
rising every time we fall.

Confucius, c. 550-478 BC
Chinese philosopher

We have forty million reasons for failure, but
not a single excuse.

Rudyard Kipling, 1865-1936
Indian-born British poet and writer

Failure is the line of least persistence.

Anonymous

Only those who dare to fail greatly can ever achieve greatly.

Robert F. Kennedy, 1925-1968
American lawyer and politician

Nothing is ever entirely wrong. Even a broken clock is right twice a day.

Anonymous

Good people are good because they've come to wisdom through failure.

William Saroyan, 1908-1981
American writer and dramatist

My downfall raises me to great heights.

Napoleon Bonaparte, 1769-1821
French emperor and general

There is no failure except in not trying.

Elbert Hubbard, 1856-1915
American writer

Faith

I believe that God is in me as the sun is in the colour and fragrance of a flower — the light in my darkness, the voice in my silence.

Helen Keller, 1880-1968
Blind and deaf American writer and scholar

Let nothing disturb you. Let nothing frighten you. Everything passes away except God.

St Theresa, 1515-1582
Spanish nun

The reason why birds can fly and we can't is simply that they have perfect faith, for to have faith is to have wings.

J. M. Barrie, 1860-1937
Scottish writer and dramatist

Faith is the subtle chain
Which binds us to the infinite; the voice
Of deep life within, that will remain
Until we crowd it thence.

Elizabeth Oakes Smith, 1806-1893
American writer

Blessed are they they that have not seen, and
yet have believed.

John 20:29

I pray hard, work hard and leave
the rest to God.

Florence Griffith Joyner, b. 1953
American track athlete

I am positive I have a soul; nor can all the
books with which the materialists have
pestered the world ever convince me of
the contrary.

Laurence Sterne, 1713-1768
Irish-born British writer

Yes, I have doubted. I have wandered off the
path. I have been lost. But I always returned. It
is beyond the logic I seek. It is intuitive — an
intrinsic, built-in sense of direction. I seem to
find my way home. My faith has wavered but
has saved me.

Helen Hayes, 1900-1993
American actress

We live in a scary horrible world now, with murder, war, poverty, hunger. I think people need to be reassured there is a higher meaning to all this chaos.

Nina Sodowski
American film producer

Faith is the bird that feels the light when the dawn is dark.

Rabindranath Tagore, 1861-1941
Indian poet and philosopher

The suffering and agonising moments through which I have passed over the last few years have also drawn me closer to God. More than ever before I am convinced of the reality of a personal God.

Martin Luther King, Jr, 1929-1968
American civil rights leader and minister

Reason is itself a matter of faith. It is an act of faith to assert that our thoughts have any relation to reality at all.

G. K. Chesterton, 1874-1936
English writer and critic

Faith builds a bridge across the gulf of death,
To break the shock blind nature cannot shun,
And lands thought smoothly on the
farther shore.

Edward Young, 1683-1765
English poet, dramatist and clergyman

With faith, man can achieve anything.
Faith is the foundation for the realisation
of God.

Sai Baba
Indian spiritual master

Faults

The greatest fault is to be conscious of none.

Thomas Carlyle, 1795-1881
Scottish historian, essayist and critic

We must touch his weaknesses with a delicate hand. There are some faults so nearly allied to excellence, that we can scarce weed out the fault without eradicating the virtue.

Oliver Goldsmith, 1728-1774
British writer

A man's faults are the faults of his time, while his virtues are his own.

Johann von Goethe, 1749-1832
German writer, dramatist and scientist

Always acknowledge a fault frankly. This will throw those in authority off their guard and give you opportunity to commit more.

Mark Twain, 1835-1910
American humorist and writer

Fear

I have not ceased being fearful, but I have
ceased to let fear control me. I have accepted
fear as a part of life — specifically the fear
of change, the fear of the unknown; and I
have gone ahead despite the pounding in
my heart that says: turn back, you'll die if
you venture too far.

Erica Jong, b. 1942
American author

Fear: the best way out is through.

Helen Keller, 1880-1968
Blind and deaf American writer and scholar

I believe anyone can conquer fear by doing
the things he fears to do, provided he keeps
doing them until he gets a record of successful
experiences behind him.

Eleanor Roosevelt, 1884-1962
*First Lady of the United States of America,
writer and diplomat*

Fear is an emotion indispensable for survival.

Hannah Arendt, 1906-1975
German-born American political philosopher

Fear is a question. What are you afraid of and why? Our fears are a treasure house of self knowledge if we explore them.

Marilyn French, b. 1929
American novelist

Within a system which denies the existence of basic human rights, fear tends to be the order of the day. Fear of imprisonment, fear of torture, fear of death, fear of losing friends, family, property or means of livelihood, fear of poverty, fear of isolation, fear of failure . . . Yet even under the most crushing state machinery, courage rises up again and again, for fear is not the natural state of civilised man.

Aung San Suu Kyi, b. 1945
*Burma's democratically elected leader and Nobel
Peace Prize winner*

Avoiding danger is no safer in the long run than outright exposure. The fearful are caught as often as the bold.

Helen Keller, 1880-1968
Blind and deaf American writer and scholar

It is not death that a man should fear, but he should fear never beginning to live.

Marcus Aurelius, 121-180 AD
Roman emperor and philosopher

Fools & Foolishness

The greatest lesson in life is to know that even fools are right sometimes.

Winston Churchill, 1874-1965
British statesman and Prime Minister

Each day, and the living of it, has to be a conscious creation in which discipline and order are relieved with some play and pure foolishness.

May Sarton, 1912-1995
American writer

Mix a little foolishness with your serious plans;
it's wonderful to be silly at the right moment.

Horace, 65-8 BC
Roman poet

If people didn't sometimes do silly things,
nothing intelligent would ever get done.

Ludwig Wittgenstein, 1889-1952
Austrian-born English philosopher

A little nonsense now and then
Is relished by the best of men.

Anonymous

Let us be grateful for the fools. But for them
the rest of us could not succeed.

Mark Twain, 1835-1910
American humorist and writer

Forgiveness

Good, to forgive,
Best, to forget!
Living, we fret;
Dying, we live.

Robert Browning, 1812-1889
English poet

Forgiveness is the key to action and freedom.

Hannah Arendt, 1906-1975
German-born American political philosopher

A quarrel between friends, when made up,
adds a new tie to friendship, as experience
shows that the callosity formed round a broken
bone makes it stronger than before.

St Francis de Sales, 1567-1622
French theologian

For my part I believe in the forgiveness of sins
and the redemption of ignorance.

Adlai Stevenson, 1900-1965
*American lawyer, statesman and
United Nations representative*

Forgive us our trespasses as we forgive them
that trespass against us.

The Lord's Prayer

The man who opts for revenge should
dig two graves.

Chinese proverb

He that cannot forgive others breaks the bridge
over which he must pass himself; for every
man has need to be forgiven.

Thomas Fuller, 1608-1661
English clergyman and writer

It is very easy to forgive others their mistakes;
it takes more grit and gumption to forgive
them for having witnessed your own.

Jessamyn West, 1907-1984
American writer

Forgiveness is not an occasional act, it is a
permanent attitude.

Martin Luther King, Jr, 1929-1968
American civil rights leader and minister

Freedom

In the future days, which we seek to make
secure, we look forward to a world founded
upon four essential freedoms. The first is
freedom of speech and expression —
everywhere in the world. The second is
freedom of every person to worship God in
his own way — everywhere in the world.
The third is freedom from want . . .
The fourth is freedom from fear.

Franklin D. Roosevelt, 1882-1945
President of the United States of America

To be free is to have achieved your life.

Tennessee Williams, 1911-1983
American dramatist

Where the spirit of the Lord is, there is liberty.

2 Corinthians, 3:17

They that can give up essential liberty to obtain a little temporary safety deserve neither liberty nor safety.

Benjamin Franklin, 1706-1790
American statesman and scientist

Free choice is the greatest gift God gives to his children.

Elisabeth Kübler-Ross, b. 1926
Swiss-born American psychiatrist

I wish that every human life might be pure transparent freedom.

Simone de Beauvoir, 1908-1986
French writer

To move freely you must be deeply rooted.

Bella Lewitzky, b. 1916
American ballet dancer

Every human being has the liberty to do that which is good, just and honest.

Anonymous

Freedom ends when it begins to deprive
another of his freedom.

Anonymous

Liberty is not a means to a higher political end.
It is itself the highest political end.

Lord Acton, 1834-1902

British political philosopher and historian

The hope of the world is still in dedicated
minorities. The trail-blazers in human,
academic, scientific and religious freedom
have always been in the minority.

Martin Luther King, Jr, 1929-1968
American civil rights leader and minister

Friendship

We are all travellers in the wilderness of this world, and the best we can find in our travels is an honest friend.

Robert Louis Stevenson, 1850-1894
Scottish writer and poet

True happiness consists not in the multitude of friends but in the worth and choice.

Ben Jonson, c. 1573-1637
English dramatist and poet

Friendship is a divine elixir that draws you towards people and allows you to spread yourself further.

Deborah Forster
Australian journalist

A real friend will tell you when you have spinach stuck in your teeth.

Anonymous

I have learned that to have a good friend is the purest of all God's gifts, for it is a love that has no exchange or payment.

Frances Farmer, 1910-1970
American actress and writer

I want someone to laugh with me, someone to be grave with me, someone to please me and help my discrimination with his or her own remark, and at times, no doubt, to admire my acuteness and penetration.

Robert Burns, 1759-1796
Scottish poet

The antidote for fifty enemies is one friend.

Aristotle, 384-322 BC
Greek philosopher

A real friend is one who walks in when the rest of the world walks out.

Walter Winchell, 1879-1972
American journalist

Friendship improves happiness and abates misery by doubling our joy and dividing our grief.

Joseph Addison, 1672-1719
English essayist

It is one of the blessings of friends that you can afford to be stupid with them.

Ralph Waldo Emerson, 1803-1882
American essayist, poet and philosopher

Fame is the scentless sunflower, with gaudy crown of gold;
But friendship is the breathing rose, with sweets in every fold.

Oliver Wendell Holmes, 1809-1894
American writer and physician

You can make more friends in two months by becoming interested in other people than you can in two years by trying to get other people interested in you.

Dale Carnegie, 1888-1955
American writer and lecturer

Friendship with oneself is all-important
because without it one cannot be friends
with anyone else in the world.

Eleanor Roosevelt, 1884-1962
*First Lady of the United States of America, writer and
diplomat*

For whoever knows how to return a kindness
he has received must be a friend above price.

Sophocles, 496-406 BC
Greek tragedian

The best mirror is an old friend.

English proverb

Anyone can sympathise with the sufferings of a
friend, but it takes a fine nature to sympathise
with a friend's success.

Oscar Wilde, 1854-1900
Irish playright, novelist and wit

If you have a friend worth loving
Love him. Yes, and let him know
That you love him, ere life's evening
Tinge his brow with sunset's glow;
Why should good words ne'er be said
Of a friend until he is dead?

Daniel W. Hoyt
Poet

I always felt that the great high privilege, relief
and comfort of friendship was that one had to
explain nothing.

Katherine Mansfield, 1888-1923
New Zealand short story writer

Under the magnetism of friendship the modest
man becomes bold; the shy, confident; the lazy,
active; or the impetuous, prudent and peaceful.

William Makepeace Thackeray, 1811-1863
English writer

True friendship is a plant of slow growth and must undergo and withstand the shocks of adversity before it is entitled to the appellation.

George Washington, 1732-1799
President of the United States of America

A friendship counting nearly forty years is the finest kind of shade-tree I know.

James Russell Lowell, 1819-1891
American poet and diplomat

Oh, the inexpressible comfort of feeling safe with a person; having neither to weigh thoughts nor measure words, but pour them all out, as they are, chaff and grain together, knowing that a faithful hand will take and sift them, keep what is worth keeping, and then, with the breath of kindness, blow the rest away.

Geoge Eliot (Mary Ann Evans), 1819-1880
English novelist

The truth is friendship is every bit as sacred and eternal as marriage.

Katherine Mansfield, 1888-1923
New Zealand short story writer

Old books, old wine, old Nankin blue,
All things, in short, to which belong
The charm, the grace, that Time makes
    strong — All these I prize, but
    (entre nous)
Old friends are best!

Henry Austin Dobson, 1840-1921
English poet

Life is nothing without friendship.

Cicero, 106-43 BC
Roman orator

To know someone here or there with whom
you feel there is understanding in spite of
distances or thoughts unexpressed — that can
make of this earth a garden.

Johann von Goethe, 1749-1832
German writer, dramatist and scientist

Think where man's glory most begins
    and ends,
And say that my glory was I had such
    friends.

W. B. Yeats, 1865-1939
Irish poet, dramatist and writer

We take care of our health, we lay up money, we make our room tight, and our clothing sufficient; but who provides wisely that he shall not be wanting in the best property of all — friends?

Ralph Waldo Emerson, 1803-1882
American essayist, poet and philosopher

If a man does not make new acquaintance as he advances through life, he will soon find himself alone. A man, sir, should keep his friendship in constant repair.

Samuel Johnson, 1709-1784
English lexicographer, essayist and wit

A friend is a present which you give yourself.

Robert Louis Stevenson, 1850-1894
Scottish writer and poet

One's friends are that part of the human race with which one can be human.

George Santayana, 1863-1952
Spanish philosopher and writer

It is the friends that you can call
at 4 a.m. that matter.

Marlene Dietrich, 1901-1992
German actress and singer

A friend is someone with whom I may be
sincere. Before him I may think aloud.

Ralph Waldo Emerson, 1803-1882
American essayist, poet and philosopher

Friendship gilds prosperity and lessens adversity
by dividing and sharing it.

Cicero, 106-43 BC
Roman orator

The most I can do for my friend is simply to
be his friend. I have not wealth to bestow
on him. If he knows that I am happy in
loving him, he will want no other reward.
Is not friendship divine in this?

Henry David Thoreau, 1817-1862
American essayist, poet and mystic

Let there be no purpose in friendship save
the deepening of the spirit.
For love that seeks aught but the disclosure
of its own mystery is not love but a
net cast forth, and only the unprofitable
is caught . . .
And in the sweetness of friendship
let there be laughter, and sharing of
pleasures.
For in the dew of little things the heart
finds its morning and is refreshed.

Kahlil Gibran, 1883-1931
Lebanese poet, artist and mystic

A companion loves some agreeable qualities
which a man may possess, but a friend loves
the man himself.

James Boswell, 1740-1795
Scottish lawyer and diarist

When befriended, remember it; when you
befriend, forget it.

Benjamin Franklin, 1706-1790
American statesman and scientist

Love is like the wild rose-briar;
Friendship like the holly tree.
The holly is dark when the rose-briar
  blooms,
But which one blooms most constantly?

Emily Brontë, 1818-1848
English novelist and poet

Life is to be fortified by many friendships.
To love and be loved is the greatest
happiness of existence.

Sydney Smith, 1771-1845
English clergyman, essayist and wit

The glory of friendship is not the outstretched
hand, nor the kindly smile, nor the joy of
companionship; it is the spiritual inspiration
that comes to one when he discovers
that someone else believes in him
and is willing to trust him.

Ralph Waldo Emerson, 1803-1882
American essayist, poet and philosopher

G

Gardens & Gardening

He who plants a garden plants happiness.

Chinese proverb

What makes a garden,
And why do gardens grow?
Love lives in gardens
God and lovers know.

Carolyn Giltinam, early 19th century
English poet

Every time I talk to a savant I feel quite sure
that happiness is no longer a possibility. Yet
when I talk to my gardener, I'm convinced of
the opposite.

Bertrand Russell, 1872-1970
English philosopher, mathematician and writer

How to be happy when you are miserable.
Plant Japanese poppies with cornflowers and
mignonette, and bed out the petunias among
the sweet-peas so they shall scent each other.
See the sweet-peas coming up.

Rumer Godden, b. 1907
English writer

God Almighty first planted a garden. And indeed it is the purest of human pleasures.

Francis Bacon, 1561-1626
English philosopher and courtier

Proceed my Friend, pursue thy healthful
    toil.
Dispose thy ground and meliorate thy soil;
Range thy young plants in walks,
    or clumps, or bow'rs,
Diffuse o'er sunny banks thy fragrant
    flow'rs:
And, while the new creation round
    thee springs,
Enjoy unchecked the guiltless bliss it brings.

John Scott, 1730-1793
British poet

A man has at least made a start in discovering the meaning of human life when he plants shade trees under which he knows full well he will never sit.

D. Elton Trueblood, b. 1900
American Quaker scholar

The planting of trees is the least self-centred of all that we can do. It is a purer act of faith than the procreation of children.

Thornton Wilder, 1897-1975
American writer

There is no unbelief:
Whoever plants a seed beneath the sod
And waits to see it push away the clod,
He trusts in God.

Elizabeth York Case, 1840-1911
American writer

Gardening is an act of grace.

May Sarton, 1912-1995
American writer and poet

Genius

A genius! For thirty-seven years I've practised fourteen hours a day, and now they call me a genius!

Pablo Sarasate, 1844-1908
Spanish violinist and composer

The secret of genius is to carry the spirit of the child into old age, which means never losing your enthusiasm.

Aldous Huxley, 1894-1963
English writer

Genius is nothing more than inflamed enthusiasm.

Anonymous

Every production of genius must be the production of enthusiasm.

Benjamin Disraeli, 1804-1881
English statesman and writer

Men give me credit for some genius. All the genius I have is this: When I have a subject in mind, I study it profoundly. Day and night it is before me. My mind becomes pervaded with it ...the effort which I have made is what people are pleased to call the fruit of genius. It is the fruit of labour and thought.

Alexander Hamilton, 1755-1804
American statesman

Often genius is just another way of spelling perseverance.

Anonymous

True genius resides in the capacity for evaluation of uncertain, hazardous and conflicting information.

Winston Churchill, 1874-1965
British statesman and Prime Minister

Everyone is a genius at least once a year; a real genius has his original ideas closer together.

George Lichtenberg, 1742-1799
German physicist, satirist and writer

The highest intellects, like the
tops of mountains, are the first to
reflect the dawn.

Lord Macaulay, 1800-1859
English historian, statesman, essayist and poet

Good sense travels on well-worn paths;
genius never.

Cesar Lombroso, 1836-1909
Italian founder of criminology

If people knew how hard I work to gain my
mastery, it would not seem so wonderful at all.

Michelangelo, 1475-1564
Italian painter and sculptor

Gifts

In all ranks of life the human heart yearns for the beautiful; and the beautiful things that God makes are his gift to all alike.

Harriet Beecher Stowe, 1811-1896
American author and social reformer

When you arise in the morning, think of what a precious privilege it is to be alive — to breathe, to think, to enjoy, to love.

Marcus Aurelius, 121-180 AD
Roman emperor and philosopher

God's gifts put man's best dreams to shame.

Elizabeth Barrett Browning, 1806-1861
English poet

Giving

A bit of fragrance always clings to the hand
that gives you roses.

Chinese proverb

Giving whether it be time, labour, affection,
advice, gifts, or whatever, is one of life's
greatest pleasures.

Rebecca Russell, b. 1905
American writer

You find true joy and happiness in life when
you give and give and go on giving.

Eileen Caddy
Co-founder of the Findhorn Foundation, Scotland

We make a living by what we get, but we make
a life by what we give.

Winston Churchill, 1874-1965
British statesman and Prime Minister

It is well to give when asked, but it is better to give unasked, through understanding.

Kahlil Gibran, 1883-1931
Lebanese poet, artist and mystic

It is more blessed to give than to receive.

Acts of the Apostles, 20:35

Not what we give, but what we share,
For the gift without the giver is bare.

James Russell Lowell, 1819-1891
American poet and diplomat

The love we give away is the only
love we keep.

Elbert Hubbard, 1856-1915
American writer

If there be any truer measure of a man than by what he does, it must be by what he gives.

Robert South, 1634-1716
English Church of England theologian

It is possible to give away and become richer. It is also possible to hold on too tightly and lose everything. Yes, the liberal man shall be rich. By watering others, he waters himself.

Proverbs 11:24, 25

A cheerful giver does not count the cost of what he gives. His heart is set on pleasing and cheering him to whom the gift is given.

Julian of Norwich
Revelations of Divine Love

The wise man does not lay up treasure. The more he gives to others, the more he has for his own.

Lao-Tze, c. 600 BC
Chinese philosopher and founder of Taoism

The heart of the giver makes the gift dear and precious.

Martin Luther, 1483-1546
German protestant reformer

He that gives should never remember; he that receives should never forget.

The Talmud

Generosity consists less of giving a great deal than in gifts well timed.

Jean de La Bruyere
French writer

The hand that gives, gathers.

English proverb

Goals

I knew I was going to be a comedian when I was about six. You get what you believe you'll get. You have to really want it and you'll get it.

Billy Connolly, b. 1942
Scottish comedian

No bird soars too high if he soars with his own wings.

William Blake, 1757-1827
English poet and artist

Far away there in the sunshine are my highest aspirations. I may not reach them but I can look up and see their beauty, believe in them and try to follow.

Louisa May Alcott, 1832-1888
American novelist

Awake, arise and stop not 'til the goal is reached.

Sai Baba
Indian spiritual leader

When goals go, meaning goes. When meaning goes, purpose goes. When purpose goes, life goes dead on our hands.

Carl Jung, 1875-1961
Swiss psychiatrist

Efforts and courage are not enough without purpose and direction.

John F. Kennedy, 1917-1963
President of the United States of America

The difference between a dream and a goal is a plan.

Anonymous

If you aspire to the highest place, it is no disgrace to stop at the second or even the third place.

Cicero, 106-43 BC
Roman orator, statesman and essayist

Aim at the sun, and you may not reach it; but your arrow will fly far higher than if you aimed at an object on a level with yourself.

Judy Hawes, b. 1913
American children's author

Set your sights high, the higher the better.
Expect the most wonderful things to happen, not in the future but right now.
Realise that nothing is too good.
Allow absolutely nothing to hamper you or hold you up in any way.

Eileen Caddy
Co-founder of the Findhorn Foundation, Scotland

Never look down to test the ground before taking your next step; only he who keeps his eye fixed on the far horizon will find his right road.

Dag Hammarskjold, 1905-1961
Swedish statesman and humanitarian

Good Points

Think of someone you admire very much.
Write down a list of the things you admire
most about this person. You have just listed
your own good points!
Read them through carefully, and give yourself
credit for having these fine qualities.

Anonymous

A man generally has the good or ill qualities he
attributes to mankind.

William Shenstone, 1714-1763
English poet

Goodness

The greatest pleasure I know is to do a good action by stealth, and to have it found out by accident.

Charles Lamb, 1775-1834
British essayist

Waste no more time arguing
what a good man should be. Be one.

Marcus Aurelius, 121-180 AD
Roman emperor and philosopher

True goodness springs from a man's heart. All men are born good.

Confucius, c. 550-c. 478 BC
Chinese philosopher

Good, the more communicated, the more abundant grows.

John Milton, 1608-1674
English poet

It was only when I lay there on rotting prison straw that I sensed within myself the first stirrings of the good. Gradually it was disclosed to me that the line separating good and evil passes, not through states, not between classes, not between political parties either, but right through every human heart and through all human hearts.

Alexander Solzhenitsyn, b. 1918
Russian writer

For the good are always merry,
Save by an evil chance,
And the merry love the fiddle,
And the merry love to dance.

W. B. Yeats, 1865-1939
Irish poet, dramatist and writer

Good is itself, what ever comes.
It grows, and makes, and bravely
Persuades, beyond all tilt of wrong;
Stronger than anger, wiser than strategy,
Enough to subdue cities and men
If we believe it with a long courage
    of truth.

Christopher Fry, b. 1909
English verse dramatist

Greatness

Great men are the guide-posts and landmarks
in the state.

Edmund Burke, 1729-1797
British statesman and philosopher

No great man lives in vain. The history of the
world is but the biography of great men.

Thomas Carlyle, 1795-1881
Scottish historian, essayist and critic

Keep away from people who try to belittle
your ambitions. Small people always do that,
but the really great make you feel that you,
too, can become great.

Mark Twain, 1835-1910
American humorist and writer

Greatness lies not only in being strong, but in
the right use of strength.

Henry Ward Beecher, 1813-1887
American clergyman

I studied the lives of great men and famous women, and I found that the men and women who got to the top were those who did the jobs they had in hand, with everything they had of energy and enthusiasm and hard work.

Harry S. Truman, 1884-1972
President of the United States of America

The heights by great men reached
  and kept
Were not attained by sudden flight,
But they, while their companions slept,
Were toiling upward in the night.

Henry Wadsworth Longfellow, 1807-1882
American poet and writer

The measure of a truly great man is the courtesy with which he treats lesser men.

Anonymous

Great lives never go out. They go on.

Benjamin Harrison, 1833-1901
President of the United States of America

Growth

Growth, in some curious way, I suspect, depends on being always in motion just a little bit, one way or another.

Norman Mailer, b. 1932
American writer

No one remains quite what he was when he recognises himself.

Thomas Mann, 1875-1955
German writer

You must learn day by day, year by year, to broaden your horizons. The more things you love, the more you are interested in, the more you enjoy, the more your are indignant about — the more you have left when anything happens.

Ethel Barrymore, 1879-1959
American actress

Women are always being tested . . . but ultimately, each of us has to define who we are individually and then do the very best job we can to grow into that.

Hillary Clinton
First Lady of the United States of America and lawyer

We learn from experiences, both good and bad, and with that knowledge comes change . . . and growth.

Anonymous

Growing up is, after all, only the understanding that one unique and incredible experience is what everyone shares.

Doris Lessing, b. 1919
British writer

Life is a lively process of becoming.

General Douglas MacArthur, 1880-1964
American military leader

Who is not satisfied with himself will grow.

Hebrew proverb

Guilt

There's no point in being crippled by guilt.
Simply acknowledge to yourself that you have
done something wrong, learn by it, and get on
with the rest of your life.

Anonymous

Should we all confess our sins to one another
we would all laugh at one another for our lack
of originality.

Kahlil Gibran, 1883-1931
Lebanese poet, artist and mystic

We all feel guilty about something. The
only positive thing about such feelings is that
they help one to change and to behave better
in the future.

Anonymous

H

Habit

Dull habit can rob you of life's rich variety.
Make a point of doing things differently sometimes. Meet some friends for breakfast, get up
early and go for an early morning walk and, in
summer, have a picnic dinner on the beach.
Life will take on a new glow.

Anonymous

Cultivate only the habits that you are willing
should master you.

Elbert Hubbard, 1856-1915
American writer

We must make automatic and habitual, as early
as possible, as many useful actions as we can.

William James, 1842-1910
American psychologist and philosopher

Happiness

Happiness must be cultivated. It is like character. It is not a thing to be safely let alone for a moment, or it will run to weeds.

Elizabeth Stuart Phelps, 1815-1852
American novelist

I don't know what your destiny will be; but one thing I know: the only ones among you who will be really happy are those who will have sought and found how to serve.

Albert Schweitzer, 1875-1965
French medical missionary

The great essentials to happiness in this life are something to do, something to love and something to hope for.

Joseph Addison, 1672-1719
English essayist

Whether happiness may come or not,
one should try and prepare one's self to
do without it.

George Eliot (Mary Ann Evans) 1819-1880
English novelist

Most people are about as happy as they make
up their minds to be.

Abraham Lincoln, 1809-1865
American statesman and President

Cherish all your happy moments: they make a
fine cushion for old age.

Booth Tarkington, 1869-1946
American writer and dramatist

Anything you're good at contributes
to happiness.

Bertrand Russell, 1872-1970
English philosopher, mathematician and writer

If only we'd stop trying to be happy, we could have a pretty good time.

Edith Wharton, 1862-1937
American novelist

Many persons have a wrong idea of what constitutes true happiness. It is not attained through self-gratification but through fidelity to a worthy cause.

Helen Keller, 1880-1968
Blind and deaf American writer and scholar

If you want to understand the meaning of happiness, you must see it as a reward and not as a goal.

Antoine de Saint-Exupery, 1900-1944
French writer and aviator

All who would win joy, must share it; happiness was born to be a twin.

Lord Byron, 1788-1824
English poet

When we cannot find contentment in ourselves, it is useless to seek it elsewhere.

Duc de la Rochefoucauld, 1613-1680
French writer

Happiness arises in the first place from the
enjoyment of one's self, and, in the next, from
the friendship and conversations of a few select
companions.

Joseph Addison, 1672-1719
English essayist

We have no more right to consume happiness
without producing it than to consume wealth
without producing it.

George Bernard Shaw, 1856-1950
Irish dramatist, writer and critic

There are eight requisites for contented living:

health enough to make work a pleasure,

wealth enough to support your needs,

strength to battle with difficulties and overcome them,

grace enough to confess your sins and forsake them,

patience enough to toil until some good is accomplished,

charity enough to see some good in your neighbour,

faith enough to make real the things of God,

hope enough to remove all anxious fear regarding the future.

Johann von Goethe, 1749-1832
German writer, dramatist and scientist

Happiness is like coke — something you get as a by-product in the process of making something else.

Aldous Huxley, 1894-1964
British novelist

The secret of happiness is not in doing what one likes, but in liking what one has to do.

J. M. Barrie, 1860-1937
Scottish writer and dramatist

Happiness is not best achieved by those who seek it directly.

Bertrand Russell, 1872-1970
British philosopher, mathematician and writer

It is neither wealth, nor splendour but tranquillity and occupation which give happiness.

Thomas Jefferson, 1743-1826
President of the United States of America

Knowledge of what is possible is the beginning of happiness.

George Santayana, 1863-1952
Spanish philosopher and writer

Hate

Hatred rarely does any harm to its object. It is the hater who suffers. His soul is warped and his life poisoned by dwelling on past injuries or projecting schemes of revenge. Rancour in the bosom is the foe of personal happiness.

Lord Beaverbrook, 1879-1964
Canadian-born British newspaper owner and writer

Hate is like acid. It can damage the vessel in which it is stored as well as destroy the object on which it is poured.

Ann Landers, b. 1918
American advice columnist

I have decided to stick with love.
Hate is too great a burden to bear.

Martin Luther King, Jr, 1929-1968
American civil rights leader and minister

If you hate a person, you hate something in him that is part of yourself. What isn't part of ourselves doesn't disturb us.

Herman Hesse, 1877-1962
German novelist and poet

Always remember that others may hate you but those who hate you don't win unless you hate them. And then you destroy yourself.

Richard M. Nixon, 1913-1994
President of the United States of America

Rather perish than hate and fear, and twice rather die than make oneself hated and feared — this must some day become the highest maxim for every single commonwealth.

Friedrich Nietzsche, 1844-1900
German philosopher

I shall never permit myself to sink so low as to hate any man.

Booker T. Washington, 1856-1915
American educator and writer

Health

I am convinced digestion is the great secret of life.

Sydney Smith, 1771-1845
English clergyman, essayist and wit

The Mind is the Key to Health and Happiness.

Sai Baba
Indian spiritual master

Cheerfulness is the best promoter of health and is as friendly to the mind as to the body.

Joseph Addison, 1672-1719
English essayist

O health! health is the blessing of the rich! the riches of the poor! who can buy thee at too dear a rate, since there is no enjoying this world without thee?

Ben Jonson, 1573-1637
English dramatist and poet

One swears by wholemeal bread, one by
sour milk; vegetarianism is the only road to
salvation of some, others insist not only on
vegetables alone, but on eating those raw . . .
The scientific truth may be put quite briefly:
eat moderately, having an ordinary
mixed diet, and don't worry.

Robert Hutchison, 1871-1960
British medical writer

The preservation of health is a duty.
Few seem conscious that there is such
a thing as physical morality.

Herbert Spencer, 1820-1903
English philosopher and journalist

Health is Wealth.
Look after it.

Sai Baba
Indian spiritual master

Heart

If a good face is a letter of recommendation, a good heart is a letter of credit.

Edward Bulwer-Lytton, 1803-1873
English novelist, dramatist and politician

The heart's affections are divided like the branches of the cedar tree; if the tree loses one strong branch, it will suffer but it does not die. It will pour all its vitality into the next branch so that it will grow and fill the empty space.

Kahlil Gibran, 1883-1931
Lebanese poet, artist and mystic

There is no better exercise for the heart than reaching down and lifting people up.

Anonymous

To put the world in order we must first put
   the nation in order;
to put the nation in order, we must first put
   the family in order;
to put the family in order, we must cultivate
   our personal life;
and to cultivate our personal life, we must
   set our hearts right.

Confucius, c. 550- c. 478 BC
Chinese philosopher

And now here is my secret, a very simple
secret; it is only with the heart that one
can see properly; what is essential is
invisible to the eye.

Antoine de Saint-Exupery, 1900-1944
French novelist and aviator

Heaven

My idea of heaven is eating foie gras to the sound of trumpets.

Sydney Smith, 1771-1845
English clergyman, essayist and wit

Grant me paradise in this world; I'm not so sure I'll reach it in the next.

Tintoretto, 1518-1594
Venetian painter

The loves that meet in Paradise shall cast out fear,
And Paradise hath room for you and me and all.

Christina Rossetti, 1830-1894
English poet

All we know
Of what they do above,
Is that they happy are, and that they love.

Edmund Waller, 1606-1687
English poet and politician

Helping

It is one of the most beautiful compensations of this life that no man can sincerely try to help another without helping himself.

Ralph Waldo Emerson, 1803-1882
American essayist, poet and philosopher

Doing nothing for others is the undoing of one's self. We must be purposely kind and generous or we miss the best part of life's existence. The heart that goes out of itself gets large and full of joy. This is the great secret of the inner life. We do ourselves most good by doing something for others.

Horace Mann, 1796-1859
American educationalist, writer and politician

If someone listens, or stretches out a hand, or whispers a word of encouragement, or attempts to understand a lonely person, extraordinary things begin to happen.

Loretta Girzatis, b. 1920
American educator and writer

Hands that help are holier than lips that pray.

Sai Baba
Indian spiritual master

When you tell your trouble to your neighbour you present him with a part of your heart. If he possesses a great soul, he thanks you; if he possesses a small one, he belittles you.

Kahlil Gibran, 1883-1931
Lebanese poet, artist and mystic

Do something for somebody every day for which you do not get paid.

Albert Schweitzer, 1875-1965
French medical missionary

No man can live happily who regards himself alone, who turns everything to his own advantage. Thou must live for another, if thou wishest to live for thyself.

Seneca, c. 4 BC - 65 AD
Roman philosopher, dramatist, poet and statesman

He who does not live in some degree for others, hardly lives for himself.

Michel de Montaigne, 1533-1592
French essayist

Only a life lived in the service of others is worth living.

Albert Einstein, 1879-1955
German-born American physicist

Home

He is happiest, be he king or peasant, who finds peace in his home.

Johann von Goethe, 1749-1832
German writer, dramatist and scientist

The ornament of a house is the friends who frequent it.

Ralph Waldo Emerson, 1803-1882
American essayist, poet and philosopher

The ideal of happiness has always taken material form in the house, whether cottage or castle; it stands for permanence and separation from the world.

Simone de Beauvoir, 1908-1986
French novelist

Seek home for rest,
For home is best.

Thomas Tusser, 1524-1580
English farmer

If you want a golden rule that will fit everybody, this is it. Have nothing in your houses that you do not know to be useful or believe to be beautiful.

William Morris, 1834-1896
English designer and craftsman

'Home' is any four walls that enclose the right person.

Helen Rowland, 1875-1950
American writer

Mid pleasures and palaces we may roam,
Be it ever so humble, there's no place
like home.

J. H. Payne, 1791-1852
American dramatist, poet and actor

The strength of a nation is derived from the
integrity of its homes.

Confucius, c. 551- c. 478 BC
Chinese philosopher

Hope

The frailest hope is better than despair.

Maria Brooks, 1795-1845
American poet

Of all the forces that make for a better world,
none is so indispensable, none so powerful as
hope. Without hope man is only half alive.

Charles Sawyer, 1887-1979
Writer

We judge of man's wisdom by his hope.

Ralph Waldo Emerson, 1803-1882
American essayist, poet and philosopher

Hope for the best, but prepare for the worst.

Proverb

Hope! of all ills that men endure
The only cheap and universal cure.

Abraham Cowley, 1618-1667
English poet and dramatist

He who has health has hope. And he who has
hope has everything.

Arabian proverb

Humour

Imagination was given to man to compensate
for what he is not, and a sense of humour to
console him for what he is.

Anonymous

A sense of humour is a sense of proportion.

Kahlil Gibran, 1883-1931
Lebanese poet, artist and mystic

The best sense of humour belongs to the man
who can laugh at himself.

Anonymous

Our five senses are incomplete without the
sixth — a sense of humour.

Anonymous

I

Ideals & Idealism

What is the use of living if it not be to strive for noble causes and to make this muddled world a better place for those who will live in it after we are gone?

Winston Churchill, 1874-1965
British statesman and Prime Minister

The ideals that have lighted my way and, time after time, have given me new courage to face life cheerfully have been Kindness, Beauty and Truth.

Albert Einstein, 1879-1955
German-born American physicist

Each time a man stands up for an ideal, or acts to improve the lot of others, or strikes out against injustice, he sends forth a tiny ripple of hope . . . and crossing each other from a million different centres of energy and daring those ripples build a current that can sweep down the mightiest walls of oppression and resistance.

Robert F. Kennedy, 1925-1968
American lawyer and politician

What do we live for, if it is not to make life less difficult for each other?

George Eliot (Mary Ann Evans), 1819-1880
English novelist

An ideal is often but a flaming vision of reality.

Joseph Conrad, 1857-1924
Polish-born English writer

Ideas

The ideas I stand for are not mine. I borrowed them from Socrates. I swiped them from Chesterfield. I stole them from Jesus. And I put them in a book. If you don't like their rules, whose would you use?

Dale Carnegie, 1888-1955
American writer and lecturer

Ideas shape the course of history.

John Maynard Keynes, 1883-1946
English economist

There's an element of truth in every idea that lasts long enough to be called corny.

Irving Berlin, 1888-1998
American composer

There is nothing in the world more powerful than an idea. No weapon can destroy it; no power can conquer it, except the power of another idea.

Anonymous

If you are possessed of an idea, you find it expressed everywhere, you even smell it.

Thomas Mann, 1875-1955
German writer

A belief is not merely an idea the mind possesses, it is an idea that possesses the mind.

Robert Bolton
English film director

Imagination

Knowledge is limited. Imagination encircles the whole world.

Albert Einstein, 1879-1955
German-born American physicist

Imagination is the beginning of creation. You imagine what you desire, you will what you imagine and at last you create what you will.

George Bernard Shaw, 1856-1950
Irish dramatist, writer and critic

Imagination finds a road to the realm of the gods, and there man can glimpse that which is to be after the soul's liberation from the world of substance.

Kahlil Gibran, 1883-1931
Lebanese poet, artist and mystic

When I examine myself and my methods of thought, I come to the conclusion that the gift of fantasy has meant more to me than my talent for absorbing positive knowledge.

Albert Einstein, 1879-1955
German-born American physicist

Imagination is the eye of the soul.

Joseph Joubert, 1754-1824
French writer and moralist

Imperfection

All things are literally better, lovelier and
more beloved for the imperfections which
have been divinely appointed, that the law
of human life may be Effort, and the law of
human judgement — Mercy.

John Ruskin, 1819-1900
English author and art critic

Independence

The greatest thing in the world is to know how
to be self-sufficient.

Michel de Montaigne, 1533-1592
French essayist

Individuality &
Conformity

Every individual human being born on this earth has the capacity to become a unique and special person, unlike any who has ever existed before or will ever exist again.

Elisabeth Kübler-Ross, b. 1926
American psychiatrist and writer

Never be afraid to tread the path alone. Know which is your path and follow it wherever it may lead you; do not feel you have to follow in someone else's footsteps.

Eileen Caddy
Co-founder of the Findhorn Foundation, Scotland

Remember always that you have not only the right to be an individual, you have an obligation to be one. You cannot make any useful contribution in life unless you do this.

Eleanor Roosevelt, 1884-1962
First Lady of the United States of America, writer and diplomat

When she stopped conforming to the conventional picture of femininity she finally began to enjoy being a woman.

Betty Friedan, b. 1921
American feminist writer

It is a blessed thing that in every age someone has had the individuality enough and the courage enough to stand by his own convictions.

Robert G. Ingersoll, 1833-1899
American lawyer, politician and writer

Don't surrender your individuality, which is your greatest agent of power, to the customs and conventionalities that have got their life from the great mass . . . Do you want to be a power in the world? Then be yourself.

Ralph Waldo Trine, 1866-1958
American poet and writer

The best things and best people rise out of their separateness; I'm against a homogenised society because I want the cream to rise.

Robert Frost, 1874-1963
American poet

Once conform, once do what other people do because they do it, and a lethargy steals over all the finer nerves and faculties of the soul. She becomes all outer show and inner emptiness: dull, callous and indifferent.

Virginia Woolf, 1882-1941
English novelist

I am still puzzled as to how far the individual counts; a lot, I fancy, if he pushes the right way.

T. E. Lawrence (Lawrence of Arabia) 1888-1935
British soldier, archaeologist and author

What's a man's first duty?
The answer's brief: to be himself.

Henrik Ibsen, 1828-1906
Norwegian writer, dramatist and poet

I didn't belong as a kid, and that always bothered me. If only I'd known that one day my differentness would be an asset, then my early life would have been much easier.

Bette Midler, b. 1945
American singer and comedian

What is right for one soul may not be right for another. It may mean having to stand on your own and do something strange in the eyes of others. But do not be daunted. Do whatever it is because you know within it is right for you.

Eileen Caddy
Co-founder of the Findhorn Foundation, Scotland

At bottom every man knows well enough that he is a unique human being, only once on this earth: and by no extraordinary chance will such a marvellously picturesque piece of diversity in unity as he is, ever be put together a second time.

Friedrich Nietzsche, 1844-1900
German philosopher

Insight

A moment's insight is sometimes
worth a life's experience.

Oliver Wendell Holmes, 1809-1894
American writer and physician

Ideas often flit across our minds more
complete than we could make them after
much labour.

Duc de la Rochefoucauld, 1613-1680
French writer

In luminous flashes of sudden vision, we may
discover jewels of wisdom hidden within
ourselves. These flashes might come in words
(a powerful phrase or poem) or in a glowing
visual image or both. When these insights
reveal themselves to us, it is as if a veil of
mist simply dropped away. Universal and
timeless truths seem to emerge from the
shadows and stand bathed in the light of
deep understanding.

Lucia Capacchione
American art therapist

Intuition

Because of their age-long training in human relations — for that is what feminine intuition really is — women have a special contribution to make to any group enterprise . . .

Margaret Mead, 1901-1978
American anthropologist and writer

Invention

To invent, you need a good imagination and a pile of junk.

Thomas Edison, 1847-1931
American inventor

Invention is a combination of brains and materials. The more brains you use, the less materials you need.

Charles F. Kettering, 1876-1958
American engineer and inventor

J

Joy

Great joy, especially after a sudden change of circumstances, is apt to be silent, and dwells rather in the heart than on the tongue.

Henry Fielding, 1707-1754
English dramatist and writer

To get the full value of joy you must have someone to divide it with.

Mark Twain, 1835-1910
American humorist and writer

Joy seems to me a step beyond happiness — happiness is a sort of atmosphere you can live in sometimes when you're lucky. Joy is a light that fills you with hope and faith and love.

Adela Rogers St John, 1894-1988
American journalist

'On with the dance! Let joy be unconfined' is my motto, whether there's any dance to dance or joy to unconfine.

Mark Twain, 1835-1910
American humorist and writer

Man only likes to count his troubles, but he does not count his joys.

Feodor Dostoevsky, 1821-1881
Russian writer

There is no such thing as the pursuit of happiness, there is only the discovery of joy.

Joyce Grenfell, 1910-1979
English actress and writer

Judgement

There is so much good in the worst of us,
And so much bad in the best of us,
That it hardly becomes any of us
To talk about the rest of us.

Anonymous

Judge a tree from its fruit: not from the leaves.

Euripides, c. 484-406 BC
Greek dramatist and poet

Why beholdest thou the mote that is in thy
brother's eye, but considerest not the beam
that is in thy own eye?

Matthew, 7:3

No man can justly censure or condemn
another, because indeed no man truly
knows another.

Thomas Browne, 1605-1682
English physician and writer

Justice

Live and let live is the rule of common justice.

Sir Roger L'Estrange, 1616-1704
French writer

Injustice anywhere is a threat to
justice everywhere.

Martin Luther King, Jr, 1929-1968
American civil rights leader and minister

The probability that we may fail in the struggle
ought not to deter us from the support of a
cause we believe to be just.

Abraham Lincoln, 1809-1865
American statesman and President

K

Kindness

Guard within yourself that treasure, kindness.
Know how to give without hesitation, how to
lose without regret, how to acquire without
meanness . . . Know how to replace in your
heart, by the happiness of those you love, the
happiness that may be wanting in yourself.

George Sand (Amandine Dupin) 1804-1876
French novelist

Perfect kindness acts without
thinking of kindness.

Lao-Tze, c. 600 BC
Chinese philosopher and founder of Taoism

Your own soul is nourished when you are kind;
it is destroyed when you are cruel.

Proverbs 11: 17

Wise sayings often fall on barren ground; but a kind word is never thrown away.

Arthur Helps, 1813-1875
English historian

When you are kind to someone in trouble, you hope they'll remember and be kind to someone else. And it'll become like a wildfire.

Whoopi Goldberg, b. 1955
American actress

So many gods, so many creeds,
So many paths that wind and wind
While just the art of being kind
Is all the sad world needs.

Ella Wheeler Wilcox, 1850-1919
American writer and poet

A good deed is never lost. He who sows courtesy reaps friendship, and he who plants kindness gathers love.

Anonymous

Knowledge

Knowledge is power itself.

Francis Bacon, 1561-1626
British philosopher, essayist and courtier

Knowledge is of two kinds. We know a subject
ourselves, or we know where we can find
information upon it.

Samuel Johnson, 1709-1784
English lexicographer, essayist and wit

Knowledge and understanding are life's
faithful companions who will never be
untrue to you. For knowledge is your
crown, and understanding your staff; and
when they are with you, you can possess
no greater treasures.

Kahlil Gibran, 1883-1931
Lebanese poet, artist and mystic

If we value the pursuit of knowledge we must be free to follow wherever that search may lead us.

Adlai Stevenson, 1900-1965
American lawyer, statesman and United Nations representative

A man's merit lies in his knowledge and deeds, not in his colour, faith, race or descent. For remember, my friend, the son of a shepherd who possesses knowledge is of greater worth to a nation than the heir to the throne, if he be ignorant. Knowledge is your true patent of nobility, no matter who your father or what your race may be.

Kahlil Gibran, 1883-1931
Lebanese poet, artist and mystic

The desire of knowledge, like the thirst of riches, increases ever with the acquisition of it.

Laurence Sterne, 1713-1768
British writer and clergyman

L

Laughter

Let there be more joy and laughter
in your living.

Eileen Caddy
Co-founder of the Findhorn Foundation, Scotland

You grow up the day you have your first real
laugh at yourself.

Ethel Barrymore, 1879-1959
American actress

Laughter gives us distance. It allows us
to step back from an event, deal with
it, and then move on.

Bob Newhart
American comedian

Laughter is a property in man
essential to his reason.

Lewis Carroll, 1832-1898
English writer, mathematician and clergyman

It is a splendid habit to laugh inwardly at
yourself. It is the best way of regaining your
good humour and of finding God without
further anxiety.

Abbé de Tourville, 1842-1903
French priest

The two best physicians of them all —
Dr Laughter and Dr Sleep.

Gregory Dean, 1907-1979
British physician

Laughter can relieve tension, soothe the pain of
disappointment, and strengthen the spirit for
the formidable tasks that always lie ahead.

Dwight D. Eisenhower, 1890-1969
American statesman and President

If you like a man's laugh before you know anything of him, you may say with confidence that he is a good man.

Feodor Dostoevsky, 1821-1881
Russian writer

When you know how to laugh and when to look upon things as too absurd to take seriously, the other person is ashamed to carry through even if he was serious about it.

Eleanor Roosevelt, 1884-1962
First Lady of the United States of America, writer and diplomat

A man isn't really poor if he can still laugh.

Anonymous

Leadership

Setting an example is not the main means of influencing another, it is the only means.

Albert Einstein, 1879-1955
German-born American physicist

The question, 'Who ought to be boss?' is like asking 'Who ought to be the tenor in the quartet?' Obviously, the man who can sing tenor.

Henry Ford, 1863-1947
American car manufacturer

Treat people as if they were what they ought to be, and you help them become what they are capable of becoming.

Johann von Goethe, 1749-1832
German writer, dramatist and scientist

Our chief want is someone who will inspire us to be what we know we could be.

Ralph Waldo Emerson, 1803-1882
American essayist, poet and philosopher

Leisure

Work is not always required . . . there is such a thing as sacred idleness, the cultivation of which is now fearfully neglected.

George MacDonald, 1824-1905
British poet and novelist

It is impossible to enjoy idling thoroughly unless one has plenty of work to do.

Jerome K. Jerome, 1859-1927
English humorous writer and novelist

To be able to fill leisure intelligently is the last product of civilisation.

Bertrand Russell, 1872-1970
English philosopher, mathematician and writer

A perpetual holiday is a good working definition of hell.

George Bernard Shaw, 1856-1950
Irish dramatist, writer and critic

Life

As long as you live, keep learning how to live.

Seneca, c. 4 BC-65 AD
Roman dramatist, poet and statesman

Is it so small a thing
To have enjoy'd the sun,
To have liv'd light
In the spring,
To have lov'd, to have thought, to have done?

Matthew Arnold, 1822-1888
English poet, essayist and educationalist

I could not, at any age, be content to take my place in a corner by the fireside and simply look on. Life was meant to be lived. Curiosity must be kept alive. The fatal thing is the rejection. One must never, for whatever reason, turn his back on life.

Eleanor Roosevelt, 1884-1962
First Lady of the United States of America, writer and diplomat

Life is a single short sentence — but I want my life to read like a beautiful sentence, one that nobody wants to end.

Neil Diamond
American singer/songwriter

Do not take life too seriously. You will never get out of it alive.

Elbert Hubbard, 1856-1915
American writer

My feeling about life is a curious kind of triumphant sensation about seeing it bleak, knowing it so, and walking into it fearlessly because one has no choice.

Georgia O'Keefe, 1887-1986
American artist

Try as much as possible to be wholly alive, with all your might, and when you laugh, laugh like hell, and when you get angry, get good and angry. Try to be alive because you will be dead soon enough.

William Saroyan, 1908-1981
American writer and dramatist

There is no cure for birth and death, save to enjoy the interval.

George Santayana, 1863-1952
Spanish philosopher and writer

It's not how things turn out — it's the joy of doing it!

Barbra Streisand, b. 1942
American singer and actress

Let your life lightly dance on the edges of Time like dew on the tip of a leaf.

Rabindranath Tagore, 1861-1941
Indian poet and philosopher

Life is good only when it is magical and musical, a perfect timing and consent, and when we do not anatomise it. You must treat the days respectfully . . . You must hear the bird's song without attempting to render it into nouns and verbs.

Ralph Waldo Emerson, 1803-1882
American essayist, poet and philosopher

The love of life is necessary to the vigorous prosecution of any undertaking.

Samuel Johnson, 1709-1784
English lexicographer, essayist and wit

The purpose of life is to matter — to count, to stand for something, to have it make some difference that we lived at all.

Leo Rosten, b. 1908
Polish-born American writer and humorist

There are two things to aim for in life: first to get what you want; and, after that, to enjoy it. Only the wisest of mankind achieve the second.

Logan Pearsall Smith, 1865-1946
American-born British wit, writer and critic

Life is a traveller on a Holy journey.

Sai Baba
Indian spiritual master

The bread of life is love, the salt of love is work, the sweetness of life is poetry, and the water of life is faith.

Anna Jameson, 1794-1860
English writer

Life is no brief candle to me, it is a sort of splendid torch which I've got hold of for the moment and I want to make it burn as bright as possible before handing it on to a future generation.

George Bernard Shaw, 1856-1950
Irish dramatist, writer and critic

At the end of your life, you will never regret not having passed one more test, not winning one more verdict or not closing one more deal. You will regret time not spent with a husband, a friend, a child or parent.

Barbara Bush, b. 1925
First Lady of the United States of America

I have never given very deep thought to a philosophy of life, though I have a few ideas that I think are very useful to me:

Do whatever comes your way to do as well as you can.
Think as little as possible about yourself.
Think as much as possible about other people.
Dwell on things that are interesting.
Since you get more joy out of giving joy to others you should put a good deal of thought into the happiness that you are able to give.

Eleanor Roosevelt, 1884-1962
First Lady of the United States of America, writer and diplomat

The most fruitful of all the arts is the art of living well.

Cicero, 106-43 BC
Roman orator

Loneliness

Always remember that you are not the only one who has ever felt rejected, unloved and lonely at some time. Reach out and help someone else in trouble, and you could be amazed at the changes in yourself — and your life!

Anonymous

If you want people to be glad to meet you, you must be glad to meet them — and show it.

Johann von Goethe, 1749-1832
German writer, dramatist and scientist

Loneliness is a state of mind.

Anonymous

Love

Great is the power of might and mind,
But only love can make us kind,
And all we are or hope to be
Is empty pride and vanity —
If love is not a part of all
The greatest man is very small.

Helen Steiner Rice, 1900-1981
American poet

The story of love is not important —
what is important is that one is capable of love.
It is perhaps the only glimpse we are permitted
of eternity.

Helen Hayes, 1900-1993
American actress

If we make our goal to live a life of
compassion and unconditional love, then the
world will indeed become a garden where all
kinds of flowers can bloom and grow.

Elisabeth Kübler-Ross, b. 1926
Swiss-born American psychiatrist and writer

Love is patient, love is kind. It does not envy, it does not boast, it is not proud. It is not rude, it is not self-seeking, it is not easily angered, it keeps no records of wrongs . . .

1 Corinthians 13: 4-5

Ego wants to get and forget,
Love want to give and forgive.

Sai Baba
Indian spiritual master

Above all, love each other deeply, because love covers over a multitude of sins.

1 Peter 4:8

There is a land of the living and a land of the dead, and the bridge is love.

Thornton Wilder, 1897-1975
American author and dramatist

Love begins when a person feels another person's need to be as important as his own.

Anonymous

Love makes all hard hearts gentle.

George Herbert, 1593-1633
English poet

Love is the only force capable of transforming
an enemy into a friend.

Martin Luther King, Jr, 1929-1968
American civil rights leader and minister

In our life there is a single colour, as on an
artist's palette, which provides the meaning of
life and art. It is the colour of love.

Marc Chagall, 1887-1985
French artist

Immature love says: 'I love you
because I need you.'
Mature love says: 'I need you
because I love you.'

Erich Fromm, 1900-1980
American psychoanalyst

One word frees us of all the weight and pain of life; that word is love.

Sophocles, 496-406 BC
Greek tragedian

All love is sweet,
Given or returned
Common as light is love,
And its familiar voice wearies not ever.

Percy Bysshe Shelley, 1792-1822
English poet

A loving heart is the truest wisdom.

Charles Dickens, 1812-1870
English writer

Love will teach us all things: but we must learn how to win love; it is got with difficulty: it is a possession dearly bought with much labour and a long time; for one must love not sometimes only, for a passing moment, but always. And let not men's sin dishearten thee: love a man even in his sin, for that love is a likeness of the divine love, and is the summit of love on earth.

Feodor Dostoevsky, 1821-1881
Russian novelist

Love is a fruit in season at all times, and within reach of every hand.

Mother Teresa of Calcutta, 1910-1997
Albanian-born missionary

To love another person is to help them love God.

Soren Kierkegaard, 1813-1855
Danish philosopher and theologian

Love comforteth like sunshine after rain.

William Shakespeare, 1564-1616
English playwright and poet

The root of the matter is a very simple and old-fashioned thing, a thing so simple that I am almost ashamed to mention it for fear of the derisive smile with which wise cynics will greet my words. The thing I mean — please forgive me for mentioning it — is love, or compassion. If you feel this, you have a motive for existence, a guide in action, a reason for courage, an imperative necessity for intellectual honesty.

Bertrand Russell, 1872-1970
English philosopher, mathematician and writer

Luck

The harder you work, the luckier you get.

Gary Player, b. 1935
South African golfer

Luck is being ready for the chance.

Anonymous

I never knew an early-rising, hard-working, prudent man, careful of his earnings, and strictly honest, who complained of bad luck.

Joseph Addison, 1672-1719
English essayist and politician

Luck is infatuated with the efficient.

Persian proverb

Good luck often has the odour of perspiration about it.

Anonymous

Shallow men believe in luck. Strong men believe in cause and effect.

Ralph Waldo Emerson, 1803-1882
American essayist, poet and philosopher

Luck is good planning, carefully executed.

Anonymous

Good luck is what a lazy man calls a hard-working man's success.

Anonymous

M

Marriage

A marriage makes of two fractional lines a whole; it give to two purposeless lives a work, and doubles the strength of each to perform it; it gives to two questioning natures a reason for living and something to live for.

Mark Twain, 1835-1910
American humorist and writer

The most important things to do in this world are to get something to eat, something to drink and somebody to love you.

Brendan Behan, 1923-1964
Irish writer

Love one another, but make not a bond
   of love;

Let it rather be a moving sea between the
   shores of your souls.
Fill each other's cup but drink not from the
   one cup.
Give one another of your bread but eat not
   from the same loaf.
Sing and dance together and be joyous, but
   let each one of you be alone.
Even as the strings of a lute are alone
   though they quiver with the same music.

Kahlil Gibran, 1883-1931
Lebanese poet, artist and mystic

A good marriage is like Dr Who's Tardis, small
and banal from the outside but spacious and
interesting from within.

Katharine Whitehorn, b. 1938
English essayist and politician

Well, what is a relationship? It's about two people having tremendous weaknesses and vulnerabilities, like we all do, and one person being able to strengthen the other in their areas of vulnerability. And vice versa. You need each other. You complete each other, passion and romance aside.

Jane Fonda, b. 1937
American actor and political activist

Love thy wife as thyself; honour her more than thyself. He who lives unmarried lives without joy . . . The children of a man who marries for money will prove a curse to him. All the blessings of a household come through the wife, therefore should her husband honour her.

The Talmud

Partnership, not dependence, is the real romance in marriage.

Muriel Fox, b. 1928
American business executive

She who dwells with me,
Whom I loved with such communion,
That no place on earth
Can ever be a solitude to me.

William Blake, 1710-1850
English poet

Men and women are made to love each other.
It's only by loving each other that they can
achieve anything.

Christina Stead, 1902-1983
Australian novelist

Let not the marriage of true minds
Admit impediments. Love is not love
Which alters when it alterations finds,
Or bends with the remover to remove.

William Shakespeare, 1564-1616
English dramatist and poet

How do I love thee? Let me count the ways.
I love thee to the depth and breadth and
height my soul can reach.

Elizabeth Barrett Browning, 1806-1861
English poet

Mind

The mind is an iceberg — it floats with only one-seventh of its bulk above water.

Sigmund Freud, 1856-1939
Austrian founder of psychoanalysis

The true, strong and sound mind is the mind that can embrace equally great things and small.

Samuel Johnson, 1709-1784
English lexicographer, essayist and wit

The mind ought sometimes to be amused, that it may the better return to thought and to itself.

Phaedrus, c. 15 BC-50 AD
Translator of Aesop's fables into Latin

Miracles

Miracles are instantaneous; they cannot be summoned but they come of themselves, usually at unlikely moments and to those who least expect them.

Katherine A. Porter, 1890-1980
American author

Miracles happen only to those who believe in them. Otherwise why does not the Virgin Mary appear to Lamaists, Mohammedans or Hindus, who have never heard of her?

Bernard Berenson, 1865-1959
American art critic

There are two ways to live your life. One is as though nothing is a miracle. The other is as though everything is a miracle.

Albert Einstein, 1879-1955
German-born American physicist

Mistakes

You know, by the time you've reached my age,
you've made plenty of mistakes if you've lived
your life properly.

Ronald Reagan, b. 1911
President of the United States of America

Anyone who has never made a mistake has
never tried anything new.

Albert Einstein, 1879-1955
German-born American physicist

Nobody makes a greater mistake than he who
does nothing because he could do so litttle.

Edmund Burke, 1729-1797
British politician

Even a mistake may turn out to be the one
thing necessary to a worthwhile achievement.

Henry Ford, 1863-1947
American car manufacturer

Morality

What is moral is what you feel good after, and what is immoral is what you feel bad after.

Ernest Hemingway, 1899-1964
American novelist

If your morals make you dreary, depend upon it, they are wrong.

Robert Louis Stevenson, 1850-1894
Scottish writer

Music

Music produces a kind of pleasure which human nature cannot do without.

Confucius, c. 550-c. 478BC
Chinese philosopher

Music has charms to soothe a savage breast.

William Congreve, 1670-1729
British dramatist

After silence, that which comes closer to
expressing the inexpressible is music.

Aldous Huxley, 1894-1963
English writer

Music religious hearts inspires;
It wakes the soul, and lifts it high,
And wings it with sublime desires,
And fits it to bespeak the Deity.

Joseph Addison, 1672-1719
English essayist

Mozart's music gives us permission to live.

John Updike, b. 1932
American novelist and poet

N

Nature

Come forth into the light of things,
Let Nature be your teacher.

William Wordsworth, 1770-1850
British poet

After you have exhausted what there is in
business, politics, conviviality, and so on —
have found that none of these finally satisfy,
or permanently wear — what remains?
Nature remains.

Walt Whitman, 1819-1892
American poet

Nature never did betray
The heart that loved her.

William Wordsworth, 1770-1850
British poet

Tune your ear
To all the wordless music of the stars
And to the voice of nature, and your heart
Shall turn to truth and goodness as the plant
Turns to the sun . . .

Ralph Waldo Trine, 1866- 1958
American poet and writer

Love all God's creation, both the whole and every grain of sand. Love every leaf, every ray of light. Love the animals, love the plants, love each separate thing. If thou love each thing thou wilt perceive the mystery of God in all; and when once thou perceive this, thou wilt thenceforth grow every day to a fuller understanding of it: until thou come at last to love the whole world with a love that will then be all-embracing and universal.

Feodor Dostoevsky, 1821-1881
Russian novelist

There is a pleasure in the pathless woods,
There is a rapture on the lonely shore,
There is society, where none intrudes,
By the deep Sea, and music in its roar:
I love not Man the less, but Nature more.

Lord Byron, 1788-1824
English poet

To see a world in a Grain of Sand,
And a Heaven in a Wild Flower,
Hold Infinity in the palm of your hand,
And Eternity in an hour.

William Blake, 1757-1827
English poet and artist

Those undescribed, ambrosial mornings when a
thousand birds were heard gently twittering
and ushering in the light, like the argument to
a new canto of an epic and heroic poem. The
serenity, the infinite promise of such a morning
...Then there was something divine and
immortal in our life.

Henry David Thoreau, 1817-1862
American essayist, poet and mystic

Pity the eye that sees no more in the sun than a stove to keep it warm and a torch to light its way between the home and business office. That is a blind eye, even if capable of seeing a fly a mile away.

Kahlil Gibran, 1883-1931
Lebanese poet, artist and mystic

All through my life, the new sights of Nature made me rejoice like a child.

Marie Curie, 1867-1934
Polish-born chemist

Every morning was a cheerful invitation to make my life of equal simplicity, and I may say innocence, with Nature herself.

Henry David Thoreau, 1817-1862
American essayist, poet and mystic

O

Obstacles

Obstacles are those frightful things you see
when you take your eyes off your goal.

Henry Ford, 1863-1947
American car manufacturer

Opportunity

All of us do not have equal talent, but all of us
should have an equal opportunity to develop
our talents.

John F. Kennedy, 1917-1963
President of the United States of America

There is no security on this earth; there is only
opportunity.

General Douglas MacArthur, 1880-1964
American military leader

God helps those that help themselves.

Benjamin Franklin, 1706-1790
American statesman and scientist

Grab a chance and you won't be sorry for a might-have-been.

Arthur Ransome, 1844-1967
British novelist

There is a tide in the affairs of men
Which, taken at the flood, leads on to
    fortune;
Omitted, all the voyage of their life
Is bound in shallows and in miseries.
On such a full sea are we now afloat,
And we must take the current when it
    serves,
Or lose our ventures.

William Shakespeare, 1564-1616
English poet and playwright

When one door closes, another opens; but often we look so long at the closed door that we do not see the one that has opened.

Anonymous

Next to knowing when to seize an opportunity, the most important thing in life is to know when to forgo an advantage.

Benjamin Disraeli, 1804-1881
British Prime Minister and writer

Great opportunities come to men who make the most of small ones.

Anonymous

Optimism

I am an optimist. It does not seem too much use being anything else.

Winston Churchill, 1874-1965
British statesman, Prime Minister and writer

One of the things I learned the hard way was that it doesn't pay to get discouraged. Keeping busy and making optimism a way of life can restore your faith in yourself.

Lucille Ball, 1911-1989
American actress

It's easy to become disheartened by the constant stream of tragedy and violence that is beamed into our living rooms, but never lose sight of the fact that many dedicated individuals and organisations are working constantly to ameliorate suffering. So next time it all seems too much to bear, focus on all the good being done by these good people.

Anonymous

All things are possible until they are proved impossible — even the impossible may only be so, as of now.

Pearl S. Buck, 1892-1972
American writer and missionary

Make the most of the best and the least of the worst.

Robert Louis Stevenson, 1850-1894
Scottish writer and poet

There is not enough darkness in the whole world to extinguish the light of one small candle.

Spanish proverb

I am an optimist, unrepentant and militant.
After all, in order not to be a fool an optimist
must know how sad a place the world
can be. It is only the pessimist who finds
this out anew every day.

Peter Ustinov b. 1921
English writer, actor and dramatist

A positive thinker does not refuse to *recognise*
the negative, he refuses to *dwell* on it. Positive
thinking is a form of thought which habitually
looks for the best results from the worst
conditions. It is possible to look for something
to build on; it is possible to expect the best for
yourself even though things look bad. And the
remarkable fact is that when you seek good,
you are very likely to find it.

Norman Vincent Peale, 1898-1993
American writer and minister

The optimist is wrong as often as is the
pessimist. But he has a lot more fun.

Anonymous

Inside my head I construct an airtight box. I keep inside it what I want to think about and everything else stays beyond the walls. . . Inside is love and friends and optimism. Outside is negativity, can't do-ism, any criticism of me and mine. Most of the time the box is as strong as steel.

Virginia Kelley
Mother of President Clinton

However much I am at the mercy of the world, I never let myself get lost by brooding over its misery. I hold firmly to the thought that each one of us can do a little to bring some portion of that misery to an end.

Albert Schweitzer, 1875-1965
French medical missionary

'Tis easy enough to be pleasant,
When life flows along like a song;
But the man worthwhile is the one
    who will smile
When everything goes dead wrong.

Ella Wheeler Wilcox, 1850-1919
American writer and poet

Two men look out between the same bars:
One sees mud, and one the stars.

Frederick Langbridge, 1849-1923
Irish religious writer

A good business manager hires optimists for
the sales department and pessimists for the
accounts department.

Anonymous

The world is changing and it is my optimistic
belief that gradually, patchily, maybe with one
step back for every two steps forward, it is
changing for the better.

Pamela Bone
Australian journalist

Originality

Every human being is intended to have a
character of his own; to be what no others are,
and to do what no other can do.

William Ellery Channing, 1780-1842
American clergyman

The merit of originality is not novelty; it is
sincerity. The believing man is the original
man; whatsoever he believes, he believes it for
himself, not for another.

Thomas Carlyle, 1795-1881
Scottish historian, essayist and critic

Originality exists in every individual because
each of us differs from the others. We are all
primary numbers divisible only by ourselves.

Jean Guitton
French writer

P

Parting

When you part from your friend, you grieve
not; for that which you love most in him may
be clearer in his absence, as the mountain to
the climber is clearer from the plain.

Kahlil Gibran, 1883-1931
Lebanese poet, artist and mystic

Adieu, adieu, kind friends, adieu, adieu, adieu,
I can no longer stay with you, stay with you.
I'll hang my harp on a weeping willow-tree,
And may the world go well with thee.

Unknown

Peace

The world will never have lasting peace so long as men reserve for war the finest human qualities. Peace, no less than war, requires idealism and self-sacrifice and a righteous and dynamic faith.

John Foster Dulles, 1888-1959
American Secretary of State

I am a man of peace. I believe in peace. But I do not want peace at any price. I do not want the peace that you find in stone; I do not want the peace that you find in the grave; but I do want the peace which you find embedded in the human breast, which is exposed to the arrows of the world, but which is protected from all harm by the power of Almighty God.

Gandhi, 1869-1948
Indian political leader

Peace is a daily, a weekly, a monthly process, gradually changing opinions, slowly eroding old barriers, quietly building new structures. And however undramatic the pursuit of peace, the pursuit must go on.

John F. Kennedy, 1917-1963
President of the United States of America

The peace of God, the peace of men,
Be upon each window, each door,
Upon each hole that lets in light,
Upon the four corners of my house,
Upon the four corners of my bed.

Gaelic blessing

Peace is not an absence of war, it is a virtue, a state of mind, a disposition for benevolence, confidence, justice.

Benedict Spinoza, 1632-1677
Dutch philosopher

Perseverance

When you get into a tight place and everything goes against you, till it seems as though you could not hang on a minute longer, never give up then, for that is just the place and time that the tide will turn.

Harriet Beecher Stowe, 1811- 1896
American author and social reformer

When I was a young man, I observed that nine out of ten things I did were failures. I didn't want to be a failure, so I did ten times more work.

George Bernard Shaw, 1856-1950
Irish dramatist, writer and critic

Winners never quit — and quitters never win.

Anonymous

By perseverance the snail reached the ark.

Charles Haddon Spurgeon, 1834-1892
British Baptist preacher

I'm extraordinarily patient, provided I get my own way in the end.

Margaret Thatcher, b. 1925
British Prime Minister

We haven't failed. We now know a thousand things that won't work, so we're that much closer to finding what will.

Thomas Edison, 1847-1931
American inventor

Never give in! Never give in! Never, never never — in nothing great or small, large or petty — never give in except to convictions of honour and good sense.

Winston Churhill, 1874-1965
British statesman and Prime Minister

Great works are performed not by strength but by perseverance.

Samuel Johnson, 1709-1784
English lexicographer, essayist and wit

If at first you don't succeed,
Try, try again.

William Edward Hickson, 1803-1870
British educationalist

Too many people let others stand in their way
and don't go back for one more try.

Rosabeth Moss Kanter, b. 1943
American writer and educator

Austere perseverance, harsh and continuous,
may be employed by the smallest of us and
rarely fails its purpose, for its silent power
grows irresistibly greater with time.

Johann von Goethe, 1749-1832
German writer, dramatist and scientist

Pleasure

Pleasure is very seldom found where it is sought; our brightest blazes of gladness are commonly kindled by unexpected sparks.

Samuel Johnson, 1709-1784
English lexicographer, essayist and wit

Give me books, fruit, French wine and fine weather and a little music out of doors, played by someone I don't know.

John Keats, 1795-1821
British poet

A book of verses underneath the Bough,
A jug of Wine, a Loaf of Bread — and Thou
Beside me singing in the Wilderness;
O! Wilderness were Paradise enow!

Omar Khayyam, 1048-1131 AD
Persian poet

Potential

If we did all the things we are capable of doing
we would truly astound ourselves.

Thomas Edison, 1847-1931
American inventor

Compared to what we ought to be we are
only half awake. We are making use of only a
small part of our physical and mental
resources. Stating the thing broadly, the human
individual thus lives far within his limits.
He possesses the power of various sorts which
he habitually fails to use.

William James, 1842-1910
American psychologist and philosopher

No matter what your level of ability, you have
more potential than you can ever develop in a
lifetime.

Anonymous

Power

The sole advantage of power is that you can do more good.

Seneca c. 4 BC-65 AD
Roman philosopher, dramatist, poet and statesman

No extraordinary power should be lodged in any one individual.

Thomas Paine, 1737-1809
English-born American revolutionary, philosopher and writer

I have never been able to conceive how any rational being could propose happiness to himself from the exercise of power over others.

Thomas Jefferson, 1743-1826
President of the United States of America

Praise

If you don't like what I do, tell me. If you like what I do, tell my boss.

Sign on department store counter

There is no such whetstone, to sharpen a good wit and encourage a will to learning, as is praise.

Roger Ascham, 1515-1568
English scholar and educationalist

It is a sure sign of mediocrity to be niggardly with praise.

Marquis de Vauvenargues, 1715-1747
French soldier and moralist

Praise is the best diet for us, after all.

Sydney Smith, 1771-1845
English clergyman, essayist and wit

Man lives more by affirmation than by bread.

Victor Hugo, 1802-1885
French poet and writer

The advantage of doing one's praising for oneself is that one can lay it on so thick and exactly in the right places.

Samuel Butler, 1835-1902
English writer

The test of any man's character is how he takes praise.

Anonymous

Prayer

Teach us to delight in simple things,
And mirth that has no bitter springs;
Forgiveness free of evil done,
And love to all men 'neath the sun.

Rudyard Kipling, 1865-1936
Indian-born British writer and poet

Who rises from Prayer a better man,
his prayer is answered.

George Meredith, 1831-1891
English poet and statesman

Prayer is the song of the heart. It reaches the
ear of God even if it is mingled with the cry
and tumult of a thousand men.

Kahlil Gibran, 1883-1931
Lebanese poet, artist and mystic

Let me be a little kinder,
Let me be a little blinder
To the faults of those around me.

Edgar A. Guest, 1881-1959
English-born American journalist, poet and author

Prejudice

Prejudices, it is well known, are most difficult to eradicate from the heart whose soil has never been loosened or fertilised by education; they grow there, firm as weeds among rocks.

Charlotte Brontë, 1816-1855
British novelist

It is never too late to give up your prejudices.

Henry David Thoreau, 1817-1862
American essayist, poet and mystic

What white people have to do is to find out in their own hearts why it is necessary to have a nigger in the first place. I'm not a nigger, I am a man, but if you think I'm a nigger, it means you need to.

James Baldwin, 1924-1987
American writer, poet and civil rights activist

Most prejudice is based upon fear of the unknown.

Anonymous

Problems

If there was nothing wrong in the world, there wouldn't be anything for us to to do.

George Bernard Shaw, 1856-1950
Irish dramatist, writer and critic

Problems are a major part of life. Don't whinge about why you always have problems. Rest assured, no matter what, throughout your life you will always have to deal with problems. So don't waste time. Get on with the solving. Take it from someone who has been there — the solving gets easier as you go along.

Sara Henderson, b. 1936
Australian outback station manager and writer

A problem well stated is a problem half solved.

Charles Franklin Kettering, 1876-1958
American engineer and inventor

It is in the whole process of meeting and solving problems that life has meaning. Problems are the cutting edge that distinguishes between success and failure. Problems call forth our courage and our wisdom; indeed, they create our courage and our wisdom. It is only because of problems that we grow mentally and spiritually. It is through the pain of confronting and resolving problems that we learn.

M. Scott Peck, b. 1936
American psychiatrist and writer

I think these difficult times have helped me to understand better than before how infinitely rich and beautiful life is in every way and that so many things that one goes around worrying about are of no importance whatsoever.

Isak Dinesen (Karen Blixen) 1885-1962
Danish writer

Those things that hurt, instruct.

Benjamin Franklin, 1706-1790
American statesman and scientist

The marvellous richness of human experience would lose something of rewarding joy if there were no limitations to overcome. The hilltop hour would not be half so wonderful if there were no dark valleys to traverse.

Helen Keller, 1880-1968
Blind and deaf American writer and scholar

Remember, without that uncomfortable bit of grit, the oyster would not produce those priceless pearls.

Anonymous

When it is dark enough, you can see the stars.

Ralph Waldo Emerson, 1803-1882
American essayist, poet and philosopher

R

Regret

I don't regret anything I've ever done, so long as I enjoyed doing it at the time.

Katharine Hepburn, b. 1909
American actress

Make it a rule of life never to regret and never look back. We all live in suspense, from day to day, from hour to hour; in other words, we are the hero of our own story.

Mary McCarthy, 1912-1989
American author and critic

Regret is an appalling waste of energy; you can't build on it; it is good only for wallowing in.

Katherine Mansfield, 1888-1923
New Zealand short story writer

Be not like him who sits by his fireside and watches the fire go out, then blows vainly upon the dead ashes. Do not give up hope or yield to despair because of that which is past, for to bewail the irretrievable is the worst of human frailties.

Kahlil Gibran, 1883-1931
Lebanese poet, artist and mystic

I have no regrets. I wouldn't have lived my life the way I did if I was going to worry about what people were going to say.

Ingrid Bergman, 1915-1982
Swedish-born American actress

There's no point dwelling on what might or could have been. You just have to go forward.

Jack Nicholson, b. 1937
American actor

You can't have rosy views about the future if your mind is full of the blues about the past.

Anonymous

Relationships

You haven't learned life's lesson very well if you haven't noticed that you can give the tone or colour, or decide the reaction you want of people in advance. It's unbelievably simple.

If you want them to take an interest in you, take an interest in them first.

If you want to make them nervous, become nervous yourself.

If you want them to shout and raise their voices, raise yours and shout.

If you want them to strike you, strike first.

It's as simple as that. People will treat you as you treat them. It's no secret. Look about you. You can prove it with the next person you meet.

Winston Churchill, 1874-1965
British statesman and Prime Minister

The world is a looking glass, and gives back to every man the reflection of his own face.

William Makepeace Thackeray, 1811-1863
British writer

A man's feeling of good-will towards others is the strongest magnet for drawing good-will towards himself.

Lord Chesterfield, 1694-1773
English statesman

We can't choose our relatives or workmates. But if you find yourself forced to put up with the company of someone who really rubs you up the wrong way, try to find something about them that you like. Then focus on that quality. You'll feel better, and the other person may even respond to your more accepting attitude.

Anonymous

People is all everything is, all it has ever been, all it can ever be.

William Saroyan, 1908-1981
American writer and dramatist

Relaxation

Treat yourself to a massage, hire a favourite video, have a hot bath and an early night, or read a book in the sun — make a point of doing something really relaxing as often as you can. It will do you no end of good physically and mentally, and will re-charge your batteries so you can face up to life's everyday challenges.

Anonymous

Religion

I love you, my brother, whoever you are — whether you worship in your church, kneel in your temple, or pray in your mosque. You and I are all children of one faith, for the diverse paths of religion are fingers of the loving hand of one Supreme Being, a hand extended to all, offering completeness of spirit to all, eager to receive all.

Kahlil Gibran, 1881-1931
Lebanese poet, artist and mystic

One's religion is whatever one is most interested in.

J. M. Barrie, 1860-1937
Scottish writer and dramatist

I am a deeply religious unbeliever.

Albert Einstein, 1879-1955
German-born American physicist

It makes all the difference in the world to your life whether you arrive at a philosophy and a religion or not. It makes the difference between living in a world which is merely a constant changing mass of phenomena and living in a significant, ordered universe.

Mary Ellen Chase, 1887-1973
American educator and author

In my religion there would be no exclusive doctrine; all would be love, poetry and doubt.

Cyril Connolly, 1903-1974
English writer, critic and literary editor

Every religion is a Lamp that illumines
the Path of Truth.

Sai Baba
Indian spiritual master

The cosmic religious experience is the
strongest and noblest driving force behind
scientific research.

Albert Einstein, 1879-1955
German-born American physicist

Responsibility

The willingness to accept responsibilty for
one's own life is the source from which self-
respect springs.

Joan Didion, b. 1935
American writer and journalist

None of us is responsible for all the things that
happen to us, but we are responsible for the
way we react to them.

Anonymous

Restrictions

Every man takes the limits of his own vision
for the limits of the world.

Arthur Schopenhauer, 1788-1860
German philosopher

I think the very restrictions which were put
on woman, which made her emphasise the
personal world, caused something very good
to be born. Whereas men dealt in terms of
nations, in terms of statistics, abstract ideology,
woman, because her world was restricted to
the personal, was more human. Now that she
is beginning to step beyond her confines, I
hope she can bring to the world the sense of
personal value of human beings, some
empathy and some sympathy.

Anaïs Nin, 1909-1977
French writer

Right

We should always do right, because it will gratify some people and astonish the rest.

Mark Twain, 1835-1910
American humorist and writer

Risk

Take calculated risks. This is quite different from being rash.

George S. Patton, 1885-1945
American military leader

Being myself includes taking risks with myself, taking risks on new behaviour, trying new ways of 'being myself', so that I can see how it is I want to be.

Hugh Prather, b. 1938
American writer

To gain that which is worth having, it may be necessary to lose everything.

Bernadette Devlin, b. 1947
Irish politician

No man is worth his salt who is not ready at all times to risk his body, to risk his well-being, to risk his life in a great cause.

Theodore Roosevelt, 1858-1919
President of the United States of America

Courageous risks are life-giving. They help you grow, make you brave and better than you think you are.

Joan L. Curcio
American educator

S

Self-acceptance

I was raised to sense what someone wanted
me to be and to be that kind of person. It
took me a long time not to judge myself
through someone else's eyes.

Sally Field, b. 1946
American actor

I was born a jackdaw; why should I be an owl?

Ogden Nash, 1902-1971
American humorous poet

There are big dogs and little dogs, but the
little dogs should not be disheartened by the
existence of the big dogs. All must bark, and
bark with the voice God gave them.

Anton Chekhov, 1860-1904
Russian dramatist and short story writer

One has just to be oneself.
That's my basic message.
The moment you accept yourself as you are,
all burdens, all mountainous burdens,
simply disappear.
Then life is a sheer joy, a festival of lights.

Bhagwan Shree Rajneesh
Indian spiritual leader

Self-confidence

I'm trying to be myself more and more. The
more confidence you have in yourself, which I
think only comes with experience and age, the
more you realise this is you and life isn't long.
So get on with it!

Kylie Minogue, b. 1968
Australian singer and actor

The important thing is not what they think of
me, it is what I think of them.

Queen Victoria, 1819-1901
British Monarch and Empress of India

Self-discipline

Some people regard discipline as a chore. For me, it is a kind of order that sets me free to fly.

Julie Andrews, b. 1934
British singer and actress

People who are unable to motivate themselves must be content with mediocrity, no matter how impressive their other talents.

Andrew Carnegie, 1835-1919
Scottish/American industrialist and philanthropist

Self-improvement

I know of no more encouraging fact than the unquestioned ability of a man to elevate his life by conscious endeavour.

Henry David Thoreau, 1817-1862
American essayist, poet and mystic

There's only one corner of the universe you can be certain of improving, and that's your own self.

Aldous Huxley, 1894-1963
English writer

Every man has to seek in his own way to make his own self more noble and to realise his own true worth.

Albert Schweitzer, 1875-1965
French medical missionary

I tell you that as long as I can conceive something better than myself I cannot be easy unless I am striving to bring it into existence or clearing the way for it.

George Bernard Shaw, 1856-1950
Irish dramatist, writer and critic

Self-knowledge

Your vision will become clear only when you can look into your heart. Who looks outside, dreams. Who looks inside, awakes.

Carl Jung, 1875-1961
Swiss psychiatrist

Your goal is to find out who you are.

A Course in Miracles

Reason is your light and your beacon of Truth. Reason is the source of Life. God has given you Knowledge, so that by its light you may not only worship him, but also see yourself in your weakness and strength.

Kahlil Gibran, 1883-1931
Lebanese poet, artist and mystic

Who in the world am I? Ah, that's the puzzle.

Lewis Carroll, 1832-1898
English mathematician and author

Resolve to be thyself; and know that he
Who finds himself, loses his misery.

Matthew Arnold, 1822-1888
British writer

To know oneself one should assert himself.

Albert Camus, 1913-1960
Algerian-born French writer

Self-respect

If you put a small value upon yourself you
can be sure that the world will not raise
your price.

Anonymous

Great God, I ask thee for no meaner pelf
Than that I may not disappoint myself.

Henry David Thoreau, 1817-1862
American essayist, poet and philosopher

To have the sense of one's own intrinsic worth, which constitutes self-respect, is potentially to have everything: the ability to discriminate, to love and to remain indifferent. To lack it is to be locked within oneself, paradoxically incapable of either love or indifference.

Joan Didion, b. 1935
American author and journalist

And above all things, never think that you're not good enough yourself. A man should never think that. My belief is that in life people will take you at your own reckoning.

Anthony Trollope, 1815-1882
British novelist

I have to live with myself, and so
I want to be fit for myself to know,
I want to be able as days go by,
Always to look myself straight in the eye.

Edgar A. Guest, 1881-1959
English-born American journalist, poet and author

Simplicity

Remember that very little is needed to
make a happy life.

Marcus Aurelius, 121-180 AD
Roman emperor and philosopher

A truly great man never puts away the
simplicity of a child.

Chinese proverb

The ability to simplify means to eliminate the
unnecessary so that the necessary may speak.

Hans Hofmann, 1880-1966
German-born American painter

Our life is frittered away by detail . . .
Simplify, simplify.

Henry David Thoreau, 1817-1862
American essayist, poet and mystic

Possessions, outward success, publicity, luxury — to me these have always been contemptible. I assume that a simple and unassuming manner of life is best for everyone, best for both the body and the mind.

Albert Einstein, 1879-1955
German-born physicist

Sisters

Sisters stand between one and life's circumstances.

Nancy Mitford, 1904-1973
English writer

Sisters, when they do get on, can be closer than anyone else; closer than parents who are apt to leave the stage halfway through the play, closer than husbands or lovers who never knew Act One. Friends can change and brothers marry. Sisters tend to stick around.

Jane Gardam, b. 1928
English novelist

I have lost such a treasure, such a sister, such a
friend as never can have been surpassed. She
was the sun of my life, the gilder of every
pleasure, the soother of every sorrow. I had not
a thought concealed from her; and it is as if I
had lost a part of myself.

Cassandra Austen
From a letter written on the death of her sister, novelist
Jane Austen, in 1817

For there is no friend like a sister
In calm and stormy weather;
To cheer one on the tedious way,
To fetch one if one goes astray,
To lift one if one totters down,
To strengthen while one stands.

Christina Rossetti, 1830-1894
English poet

Solitude

Loneliness is the poverty of self; solitude is the
richness of self.

May Sarton, 1912-1995
American writer and poet

I was never less alone than when by myself.

Edward Gibbon, 1737-1794
English historian and politician

In solitude we give passionate attention
to our lives, to our memories, to the
details around us.

Virginia Woolf, 1882-1941
English novelist

Arranging a bowl of flowers in the
morning can give a sense of quiet in a crowded
day — like writing a poem or saying a prayer.
What matters is that one be for a time
inwardly attentive.

Anne Morrow Lindbergh, b. 1906
American writer

The best thinking has been done in solitude.
The worst has been done in turmoil.

Thomas Edison, 1847-1931
American inventor

The more powerful and original a mind, the
more it will incline to the religion of solitude.

Aldous Huxley, 1894-1963
English writer

Sorrow

The deeper the sorrow that carves into your
being, the more joy you can contain. Joy and
sorrow are inseparable.

Kahlil Gibran, 1883-1931
Lebanese poet, artist and mystic

Sorrows are our best educators. A man
can see further through a tear than through
a telescope.

Anonymous

Happiness is beneficial for the body, but it is grief that develops the powers of the mind.

Marcel Proust, 1871-1922
French writer

Where there is sorrow there is holy ground.

Oscar Wilde, 1854-1900
Irish dramatist, novelist and wit

The groundwork of life is sorrow. But that once established one can start to build. And until that is established one can build nothing: no life of any sort.

D. H. Lawrence, 1855-1930
British writer, poet and critic

Have courage for the greatest sorrows of life and patience for the small ones, and when you have laboriously accomplished your daily tasks, go to sleep in peace. God is awake.

Victor Hugo, 1802-1885
French poet and writer

Strength

If we are strong, our strength will
speak for itself.
If we are weak, words will be no help.

John F. Kennedy, 1917-1963
President of the United States of America

Our strength lies, not alone in our proving
grounds and our stockpiles, but in our ideals,
our goals and their universal appeal to all men
who are struggling to breathe free.

Adlai Stevenson, 1900-1965
*American statesman, lawyer and United Nations
representative*

Decision is one of the duties of strength.

H. G. Wells, 1866-1946
English writer

Success

Success is all about the quiet accumulation
of small triumphs.

J. P. Donleavy, b. 1926
Irish-born American writer and dramatist

There are two kinds of success. One is the very
rare kind that comes to the man who has the
power to do what no one else has the power to
do. That is genius. But the average man who
wins what we call success is not a genius. He is
a man who has merely the ordinary qualities
that he shares with his fellows, but who has
developed those ordinary qualities to a more
than ordinary degree.

Theodore Roosevelt, 1858-1919
President of the United States of America

We are prone to judge success by the index of
our salaries or the size of our automobiles,
rather than by the quality of our service and
our relationship to humanity.

Martin Luther King, Jr, 1929-1968
American civil rights leader and minister

A minute's success pays the failure of years.

Robert Browning, 1812-1889
English poet

I hope I have convinced you — the only
thing that separates successful people from
the ones who aren't is the willingness to work
very, very hard.

Helen Gurley Brown, b. 1922
American publisher and author

Success is not about money and power. Real
success is about relationships. There's no point
in making $50 million a year if your teenager
thinks you're a jerk and you spend no time
with your wife.

Christopher Reeve, b. 1952
American screen actor

The secret of success is constance to purpose.

Benjamin Disraeli, 1804-1881
British Prime Minister and writer

Self-trust is the first secret of success.

Ralph Waldo Emerson, 1803-1882
American essayist, poet and philosopher

Eighty percent of success is showing up.

Woody Allen, b. 1935
American film director, writer and comedian

The difference between failure and success is doing a thing nearly right and doing a thing exactly right.

Anonymous

My formula for success? Rise early, work late, strike oil.

John Paul Getty, 1892-1976
American oil magnate

The men I have seen succeed have always been cheerful and hopeful, who went about their business with a smile on their faces, and took all the changes and chances to this mortal life like men.

Charles Kingsley, 1819-1875
English writer, poet and clergyman

Success is a state of mind. If you want success, start thinking of yourself as a success.

Anonymous

You must never conclude, even though everything goes wrong, that you cannot succeed. Even at the worst there is a way out, a hidden secret that can turn failure into success and despair into happiness. No situation is so dark that there is not a ray of light.

Norman Vincent Peale, 1898-1993
American writer and minister

Half the things that people do not succeed in, are through the fear of making the attempt.

James Northcote, 1746-1831
English painter

The secret of success is to do the common things uncommonly well.

John D. Rockefeller, 1839-1937
American oil magnate and philanthropist

To succeed in the world we must do all we can to appear successful.

Duc de La Rochefoucauld, 1613-1680
French writer

One only gets to the top rung on the ladder by steadily climbing up one at a time, and suddenly all sorts of powers, all sorts of abilities which you thought never belonged to you — suddenly become within your own possibility and you think, 'Well, I'll have a go, too.'

Margaret Thatcher, b. 1925
British Prime Minister

As is the case in all branches of the arts, success depends in a very large measure upon individual initiative and exertion, and cannot be achieved except by dint of hard work.

Anna Pavlova, 1881-1931
Russian ballet dancer

Do your work with your whole heart and you will succeed — there is so little competition.

Elbert Hubbard, 1856-1915
American writer

There are many paths to the top of the mountain, but the view is always the same.

Chinese proverb

It's Up To You!

If you think you're a winner you'll win.
If you dare to step out you'll succeed.
Believe in your heart, have a purpose to
　start.
Aim to help fellow man in his need.
Thoughts of faith must replace every doubt.
Words of courage and you cannot fail.
If you stumble and fall, rise and stand ten
　feet tall,
You determine the course that you sail.

Anonymous

Suffering

A man who fears suffering is already suffering
from what he fears.

Michel de Montaigne, 1533-1592
French essayist and moralist

Recognising the necessity for suffering I have
tried to make of it a virtue. If only to save
myself from bitterness, I have attempted to see
my personal ordeals as an opportunity to transform myself and heal the people involved in
the tragic situation which now obtains. I have
lived these past few years with the conviction
that unearned suffering is redemptive.

Martin Luther King, Jr, 1929-1968
American civil rights leader and minister

Although the world is very full of suffering, it
is also full of the overcoming of it.

Helen Keller, 1880-1968
Blind and deaf American writer and scholar

Never to suffer would have been never to have been blessed.

Edgar Allan Poe, 1809-1849
American poet and writer

Strength is born in the deep silence of long-suffering hearts; not amid joy.

Felicia Hemans, 1793-1835
British poet

Who will tell whether one happy moment of love, or the joy of breathing or walking on a bright morning and smelling the fresh air, is not worth all the suffering and effort which life implies?

Erich Fromm, 1900-1980
American psychoanalyst

Sympathy

Sympathy is the golden key that unlocks the hearts of others.

Anonymous

Pity may represent no more than the impersonal concern which prompts the mailing of a cheque, but true sympathy is the personal concern which demands the giving of one's soul.

Martin Luther King, Jr, 1929-1968
American civil rights leader and minister

Sympathy is thinking with your heart.

Anonymous

T

Tact

Silence is not always tact, and it is tact that is golden, not silence.

Samuel Butler, 1835-1902
English writer

Tact is the ability to describe others as they see themselves.

Abraham Lincoln, 1809-1865
American statesman and President

In the battle of existence, talent is the punch; tact is the clever footwork.

Wilson Mizner, 1876-1933
American writer, wit and dramatist

Thought

Few people think more than two or three times a year. I have made an international reputation for myself by thinking once or twice a week.

George Bernard Shaw, 1856-1950
Irish dramatist, writer and critic

Great thoughts come from the heart.

Marquis de Vauvenargues, 1715-1747
French soldier and writer

As soon as man does not take his existence for granted, but beholds it as something unfathomably mysterious, thought begins.

Albert Schweitzer, 1875-1965
French medical missionary

All that we are is the result of what we have thought; it is founded on our thoughts, it is made up of our thoughts. If a man speaks or acts with a pure thought, happiness follows him, like a shadow that never leaves him.

Buddha, 563-483 BC
Indian religious teacher and founder of Buddhism

Thinking is the talking of the soul with itself.

Plato, c. 429-347 BC
Greek philosopher

It is not best that we should all think alike; it is difference of opinion which makes horse races.

Mark Twain, 1835-1910
American humorist and writer

Time

The moment passed is no longer; the future may never be; the present is all of which man is master.

Jean-Jacques Rousseau, 1712-1778
Swiss-born French philosopher and essayist

Oh, be swift to love! Make haste to be kind. Do not delay; the golden moments fly!

Henry Wadsworth Longfellow, 1807-1882
American poet and writer

A man who dares waste one hour of time has not discovered the value of life.

Charles Darwin, 1809-1882
English naturalist

In reality, killing time
Is only the name for another
of the multifarious ways
By which time kills us.

Sir Osbert Sitwell, 1892-1969
English poet and writer

Enjoy the present hour,
Be thankful for the past,
And neither fear nor wish
Th' approaches of the last.

Abraham Cowley, 1618-1667
English poet and dramatist

Tolerance

All human beings are born free and equal
in dignity and rights.

Universal Declaration of Human Rights

Understanding everything makes one
very tolerant.

Mme Anne de Staël, 1766-1817
Swiss-born French writer

If you cannot mould yourself as you would
wish, how can you expect other people to be
entirely to your liking?

Thomas à Kempis, c. 1380-1471
German monk

No man can justly censure or condemn
another, indeed no man truly knows another.

Sir Thomas Browne, 1605-1682
English physician and writer

You have no idea of the tremendous release and deep peace that comes from meeting yourself and your brothers totally without judgement.

A Course in Miracles

We must respect the other fellow's religion, but only in the sense and to the extent that we respect his theory that his wife is beautiful and his children smart.

H. L Mencken, 1880-1956
American writer, critic and satirist

O God, help us not to despise or oppose what we do not understand.

William Penn, 1644-1718
English Quaker and founder of Pennsylvania

One ought to examine himself for a very long time before thinking of condemning others.

Molière, 1622-1673
French dramatist and actor

Travel

Travelling and freedom are perfect
partners and offer an opportunity to grow
in new dimensions.

Donna Goldfein, b. 1933
American writer

Keep things on your trip in perspective, and
you'll be amazed at the perspective you gain on
things back home while you're away . . . One's
little world is put into perspective by the
bigger world out there.

Gail Rubin Bereny, b. 1942
American writer

Give me the clear blue sky over my head, and
the green turf beneath my feet, a winding road
before me, and a three hours' march to dinner.

William Hazlitt, 1778-1830
British essayist

The wise man travels to discover himself.

James Russell Lowell, 1819-1891
American poet and diplomat

For my part, I travel not to go anywhere, but to go. I travel for travel's sake. The great affair is to move.

Robert Louis Stevenson, 1850-1894
Scottish writer and poet

A traveller. I love his title. A traveller is to be reverenced as such. His profession is the best symbol of our life. Going from — toward; it is the history of every one of us.

Henry David Thoreau, 1817-1862
American essayist, poet and mystic

One of the pleasantest things in the world is going on a journey; but I like to go by myself.

William Hazlitt, 1778-1830
British essayist

Truth

Truth never damages a cause that is just.

Gandhi, 1869-1948
Indian political leader

The pursuit of truth shall set you free — even if you never catch up with it.

Clarence Darrow, 1857-1938
American lawyer, writer and reformer

Half the misery in the world comes of want of courage to speak and to hear the truth plainly, and in a spirit of love.

Harriet Beecher Stowe, 1811-1896
American author and social reformer

Ethical axioms are found and tested not very differently from the axioms of science. Truth is what stands the test of experience.

Albert Einstein, 1879-1955
German-born American physicist

The best test of truth is the power of the thought to get itself accepted in the competition of the market.

Oliver Wendell Holmes, 1809-1894
American writer and physician

If you tell the truth you don't have to remember anything.

Mark Twain, 1835-1910
American humorist and writer

I never give them hell. I just tell the truth and they think it's hell.

Harry S. Truman, 1884-1972
American statesman and President

God offers to every mind its choice between truth and repose.

Ralph Waldo Emerson, 1803-1882
American essayist, poet and philosopher

There are no new truths, but only truths that have been recognised by those who have perceived them without noticing.

Mary McCarthy, 1912-1989
American writer

It is the calling of great men, not so much to preach new truths, as to rescue from oblivion those old truths which it is our wisdom to remember and our weakness to forget.

Sydney Smith, 1771-1845
English essayist, clergyman and wit

U

Understanding

Everything that I understand, I understand only because I love.

Leo Tolstoy, 1828-1910
Russian writer

I have striven not to laugh at human actions, not to weep at them, nor to hate them, but to understand them.

Benedict Spinoza, 1632-1677
Dutch philosopher

Unity

United we stand, divided we fall.

English proverb

V

Victory

Victory — a matter of staying power.

Elbert Hubbard, 1856-1915
American writer

Victory at all costs, victory in spite of terror, victory no matter how long and hard the road may be; for without victory there is no survival.

Winston Churchill, 1874-1965
British statesman and Prime Minister

In war there is no substitute for victory.

General Douglas MacArthur, 1880-1964
American military leader

Virtue

A virtue to be serviceable must, like gold,
be alloyed with some commoner but more
durable metal.

Samuel Butler, 1835-1902
English writer

Virtue is its own reward.

John Dryden, 1631-1700
English poet, satirist and dramatist

No one gossips about other
people's secret virtues.

Bertrand Russell, 1872-1970
English philosopher, mathematician and writer

Virtue, perhaps, is nothing more than
politeness of the soul.

Honoré de Balzac, 1799-1850
French writer

Vocation

Each honest calling, each walk of life, has its own elite, its own aristocracy based upon excellence of performance.

James Bryant Conant
Writer

Every calling is great when greatly pursued.

Oliver Wendell Holmes, 1809-1894
American writer and physician

It is well for a man to respect his own vocation whatever it is and to think himself bound to uphold it and to claim for it the respect it deserves.

Charles Dickens, 1812-1870
English writer

Walking

Walking is man's best medicine.

Hippocrates, c. 460-c. 377 BC
Greek physician

Walking not only strengthens the muscles and bones and is good for the heart and digestion, it also relaxes the mind and soothes the spirit. And it doesn't cost a thing. All you need is a pair of comfortable shoes (essential) and a dog (optional). So what are you waiting for? Take at least three long walks a week, and you'll soon be hooked.

Anonymous

Walking is the best possible exercise. Habituate yourself to walk very far.

Thomas Jefferson, 1743-1826
President of the United States of America

Wealth

Riches are for spending.

Francis Bacon, 1561-1626
British philosopher, essayist and courtier

I've been rich and I've been poor;
rich is better.

Sophie Tucker, 1884-1966
American singer

Few rich men own their own property. The
property owns them.

Robert G. Ingersoll, 1833-1899
American lawyer, orator and writer

Increase of material comforts, it may be
generally laid down, does not in any way
whatsoever conduce to moral growth.

Gandhi, 1869-1948
Indian political leader

Unto whomsoever much is given, of him shall
be much required.

St Luke 12:48

Money can't buy happiness, but it
can buy freedom.

Anonymous

Riches are chiefly good because they
give us time.

Charles Lamb, 1775-1834
English essayist

Wealth may be an excellent thing, for it means
power, it means leisure, it means liberty.

James Russell Lowell, 1819-1891
American poet and diplomat

One can never really be too thin or too rich.

Wallis Simpson, Duchess of Windsor, 1896-1986
American socialite and wife of the Duke of Windsor

Riches do not consist in the possession of
treasures but in the use of them.

Napoleon Bonaparte, 1769-1821
French emperor and general

Life's greatest riches have nothing to
do with money.

Anonymous

The day, water, sun, moon, night — I do not
have to purchase these things with money.

Titus Maccius Plautus, c. 254-184 BC
Roman dramatist

Wisdom

Wisdom is to live in the present, plan for the future and profit from the past.

Anonymous

Wisdom is the right use of knowledge. To know is not to be wise. Many men know a great deal, and are all the greater fools for it. There is no fool so great as the knowing fool. But to know how to use knowledge is to have wisdom.

Charles Haddon Spurgeon, 1834-1892
British Baptist preacher

Blessed is the man who finds wisdom, the man who gains understanding, for he is more profitable than silver and yields better returns than gold.

Proverbs 3:13-15

Keep me away from the wisdom which
does not cry, the philosophy which does
not laugh and the greatness which does
not bow before children.

Kahlil Gibran, 1883-1931
Lebanese poet, artist and mystic

By three methods may we learn wisdom: first,
by reflection, which is noblest; second, by
imitation, which is easiest; and third,
by experience, which is the bitterest.

Confucius, c.550-478 BC
Chinese philosopher

The growth of wisdom may be gauged exactly
by the diminution of ill-temper.

Friedrich Nietzsche, 1844-1900
German philosopher

The most manifest sign of wisdom is a
continual cheerfulness; a state like that
in the regions above the moon, always
clear and calm.

Michel de Montaigne, 1533-1592
French essayist

Wonder

For a man who cannot wonder is but a pair of spectacles behind which there are no eyes.

Thomas Carlyle, 1795-1881
Scottish historian, essayist and critic

If I had influence with the good fairy who is supposed to preside over the christening of all children, I should ask that her gift to each child in the world be a sense of wonder so indestructible that it would last throughout life.

Rachel Carson, 1907-1964
American writer and biologist

Tyger! Tyger! burning bright
In the forests of the night,
What immortal hand or eye
Could frame thy fearful symmetry?

William Blake, 1757-1827
English poet and artist

The world will never starve for want of
wonders; but only for want of wonder.

G.K. Chesterton, 1874-1936
English writer, poet and critic

It is a wholesome and necessary thing for
us to turn again to the earth and in the
contemplation of her beauties to know the
sense of wonder and humility.

Rachel Carson, 1907-1964
American writer and biologist

I am so absorbed in the wonder of earth and
the life upon it that I cannot think of heaven
and the angels. I have enough for this life.

Pearl S. Buck, 1892-1972
American writer and missionary

Work

Thank God — every morning when you get up — that you have something to do which must be done, whether you like it or not. Being forced to work, and forced to do your best, will breed in you a hundred virtues which the idle will never know.

Charles Kingsley, 1819-1875
English writer, poet and clergyman

Who said you should be happy? Do your work.

Colette, 1873-1954
French writer

Each morning sees some task begun,
Each evening sees its close.
Something attempted, something done,
Has earned a night's repose.

Henry Wadsworth Longfellow, 1807-1882
American poet and writer

Laziness may appear attractive, but work gives satisfaction.

Anne Frank, 1929-1945
Dutch schoolgirl diarist and victim of the Nazis

Work saves us from three great evils: boredom, vice and need.

Voltaire, 1694-1778
French writer, poet and philosopher

If you can't get the job you want, accept any work you can get and do your very best. You could be surprised where it leads.

Anonymous

What is the use of health, or of life, if not to do some work therewith?

Thomas Carlyle, 1795-1881
Scottish historian, essayist and critic

Work is much more fun than fun.

Noel Coward, 1899-1973
English dramatist, actor and composer

My grandfather once told me there were two kinds of people: those who do the work and those who take the credit. He told me to try to be in the first group — there was much less competition.

Indira Gandhi, 1917-1984
Prime Minister of India

Hire yourself out to work that is beneath you rather than become dependent on others.

The Talmud

I long to accomplish a great and noble task, but it is my chief duty to accomplish small tasks as if they were great tasks.

Helen Keller, 1850-1968
Blind, deaf American writer and scholar

Career is too pompous a word. It was a job, and I have always felt privileged to be paid for what I love doing.

Barbara Stanwyck, 1907-1990
American screen actress

There is no point in work unless it absorbs you like an absorbing game. It if doesn't absorb you, if it's never any fun, don't do it.

D. H. Lawrence, 1885-1930
British writer, poet and critic

My father taught me to work, but not to love it. I never did like to work, and I don't deny it. I'd rather read, tell stories, crack jokes, talk, laugh — anything but work.

Abraham Lincoln, 1809-1865
American statesman and President

Work is the grand cure of all the maladies and miseries that ever beset mankind.

Thomas Carlyle, 1795-1881
Scottish historian and essayist

Without work all life goes rotten.

Albert Camus, 1913-1960
Algerian-born French writer

No man needs sympathy because he has to work . . . Far and away the best prize that life offers is the chance to work hard at work worth doing.

Theodore Roosevelt, 1858-1919
President of the United States of America

Worry

What's the use of worrying?
It never was worthwhile,
So, pack up your troubles in your old kit-bag,
And smile, smile, smile.

George Asaf, 1880-1951
American songwriter

The reason why worry kills more people than work is that more people worry than work.

Robert Frost, 1874-1963
American poet

When I look back on all these worries I remember the story of the old man who said on his deathbed that he had had a lot of trouble in his life, most of which never happened.

Winston Churchill, 1874-1965
British statesman and Prime Minister

There are no troubles in my life except the troubles inseparable from being a spirit living in the flesh.

George Santayana, 1863-1952
Spanish philosopher and writer

Worth

A man passes for what he is worth. What he is engraves itself on his face in letters of light.

Ralph Waldo Emerson, 1803-1882
American essayist, poet and philosopher

Y

Yesterday, Today & Tomorrow

Today is yesterday's pupil.

Thomas Fuller, 1608-1661
English clergyman and writer

I've shut the door on yesterday
And thrown the key away —
Tomorrow has no fears for me,
Since I have found today.

Vivian Y. Laramore
American poet

Light tomorrow with today.

Elizabeth Barrett Browning, 1806-1861
English poet

Finish every day and be done with it. You have done what you could. Some blunders and absurdities no doubt crept in; forget them as soon as you can. Tomorrow is a new day; begin it well and serenely and with too high a spirit to be cumbered with your old nonsense. This day is all that is good and fair. It is too dear, with its hopes and invitations, to waste a moment on yesterdays.

Ralph Waldo Emerson, 1803-1882
American essayist, poet and philosopher

Yesterday is a cancelled cheque.
Tomorrow is a promissory note.
Today is ready cash. Use it!

Anonymous

Out of Eternity the new Day is born;
Into Eternity at night will return.

Thomas Carlyle, 1795-1851
Scottish historian, essayist and critic

Do not ask what tomorrow may bring, and count as profit every day that Fate allows.

Horace 65-8 BC
Roman poet

Write in your heart that every day is the best day of the year.

Ralph Waldo Emerson, 1803-1882
American essayist, poet and philosopher

Redeem thy misspent time that's past;
Live this day as if 'twere thy last.

Thomas Ken, 1637-1711
English bishop

As yesterday is history and tomorrow may never come, I have resolved from this day on, I will do all the business I can honestly, have all the fun I can reasonably, do all the good I can do willingly, and save my digestion by thinking pleasantly.

Robert Louis Stevenson, 1850-1894
Scottish writer and poet

Tomorrow is the most important thing in life. Comes into us at midnight very clean. It's perfect when it arrives and it puts itself in our hands. It hopes we've learned something from yesterday.

John Wayne, 1907-1979
American screen actor

The only limit to our realisation of tomorrow will be our doubts of today. Let us move forward with strong and active faith.

Franklin D. Roosevelt, 1882-1945
President of the United States of America

You

Start treating yourself as if you are the most important asset you'll ever have. After all, aren't you?

Anonymous

Be yourself. Nobody is better qualified.

Anonymous

Our problem is that we make the mistake of comparing ourselves with other people. You are not inferior or superior to any human being . . . You do not determine your success by comparing yourself to others, rather you determine your success by comparing your accomplishments to your capabilities. You are 'number one' when you do the best you can with what you have, every day.

Zig Siglar
American motivational writer

Youth

Youth is the time to go flashing from one end of the world to the other . . . to try the manners of different nations; to hear the chimes at midnight; to see the sunrise in town and country; to be converted at a revival; to circumnavigate metaphysics; write halting verses; run a mile to see a fire, and wait all day long in the theatre to applaud *Hernani*.

Robert Louis Stevenson, 1850-1894
Scottish writer and poet

Youth is happy because it has the ability to see beauty. Anyone who keeps the ability to see beauty never grows old.

Franz Kafka, 1883-1924
Austrian novelist

On with the dance! Let joy be unconfined;
No sleep till morn when Youth and Pleasure meet
To chase the glowing Hours with flying feet.

Lord Byron, 1788-1821
English poet

In case you're worried about what's going to become of the younger generation, it's going to grow up and start worrying about the younger generation.

Anonymous

It takes a lifetime to become young.

Pablo Picasso, 1881-1973
Spanish artist

The real lost souls don't wear their hair long and play guitars. They have crew cuts, trained minds, sign on for research on biological warfare, and don't give their parents a moment's worry.

J. B. Priestley, 1894-1984
English writer and dramatist

Z

Zeal

Through zeal, knowledge is gained, through lack of zeal, knowledge is lost. Let a man who knows this double path of gain and loss thus place himself that knowledge may grow.

Buddha, 563-483 BC
Indian religious teacher and founder of Buddhism

Subject Index

Write down your own
Pocket Positives

*Write down your own
Pocket Positives*

Write down your own
Pocket Positives

*Write down your own
Pocket Positives*

Write down your own
Pocket Positives

Write down your own
Pocket Positives

*Write down your own
Pocket Positives*

*Write down your own
Pocket Positives*